# The God of All Comfort

*and the Secret of His Comforting*

By Hannah Whitall Smith

Published by Pantianos Classics

ISBN-13: 978-1975674359

First published in 1906

# Contents

# Chapter One - Why This Book Has Been Written

*"My heart is inditing a good matter; I speak of the things which I have made touching the king."*

I was once talking on the subject of religion with an intelligent agnostic, whom I very much wished to influence, and after listening to me politely for a little while, he said, "Well, madam, all I have to say is this. If you Christians want to make us agnostics inclined to look into your religion, you must try to be more comfortable in the possession of it yourselves. The Christians I meet seem to me to be the very most uncomfortable people anywhere around. They seem to carry their religion as a man carries a headache. He does not want to get rid of his head, but at the same time it is very uncomfortable to have it. And I for one do not care to have that sort of religion."

This was a lesson I have never forgotten, and it is the primary cause of my writing this book.

I was very young in the Christian life at the time of this conversation, and was still in the first joy of my entrance into it, so I could not believe that any of God's children could be as uncomfortable in their religious lives as my agnostic friend had asserted. But when the early glow of my conversion had passed, and I had come down to the dullness of everyday duties and responsibilities, I soon found from my own experience, and also from the similar experiences of most of the Christians around me, that there was far too much truth in his assertion, and that the religious life of most of us was full of discomfort and unrest. In fact, it seemed, as one of my Christian friends said to me one day when we were comparing our experiences, "as if we had just enough religion to make us miserable."

I confess that this was very disappointing, for I had expected something altogether different. It seemed to me exceedingly incongruous that a religion, whose fruits were declared in the Bible to be love, and joy, and peace should so often work out practically in an exactly opposite direction, and should develop the fruits of doubt, and fear, and unrest, and conflict, and discomforts of every kind; and I resolved if possible to find out what was the matter. Why, I asked myself, should the children of God lead such utterly uncomfortable religious lives when He has led us to believe that His yoke would be easy and His burden light? Why are we tormented with so many spiritual doubts, and such heavy spiritual anxieties? Why do we find it so hard to be sure that God really loves us, and why is it that we never seem able to believe long at a time in His kindness and His care? How is it that we can let ourselves suspect Him of forgetting us and forsaking us in times of need? We can trust our earthly friends, and can be comfortable in their companionship, and why is it then that we cannot trust our heavenly Friend, and that we seem unable to be comfortable in His service?

I believe I have found the answer to these questions, and I should like to state frankly that my object in writing this book is to try to bring into some troubled Christian lives around me a little real and genuine comfort. My own idea of the religion of the Lord Jesus Christ is that it was meant to be full of comfort. I feel sure any unprejudiced reader of the New Testament would say the same; and I believe that every newly converted soul, in the first joy of its conversion, fully expects it. And yet, as I have said, it seems as if, with a large proportion of Christians, their religious lives are the most uncomfortable part of their existence. Does the fault of this state of things lie with the Lord? Has He promised more than He is able to supply?

A writer has said, "We know what overadvertisement is. It is a twentieth-century disease from which we all suffer. There are posters on every billboard, exaggerations on every blank wall, representations and misrepresentations without number. What visions we have seen of impossible fruits and flowers grown from Mr. So-and-So's seeds. Everything is overadvertised. Is it the same with the kingdom of God? Do the fruits which we raise from the good seed of the kingdom verify the description given by Him from whom we obtained that good seed? Has He played us false? There is a feeling abroad that Christ has offered in His Gospel more than He has to give. People think that they have not exactly realized what was predicted as the portion of the children of God. But why is this so? Has the kingdom of God been overadvertised, or is it only that it has been underbelieved; has the Lord Jesus Christ been overestimated, or has He only been undertrusted?"

What I want to do in this book is to show, in my small measure, what I firmly believe, that the kingdom of God could not possibly be overadvertised, nor the Lord Jesus Christ overestimated, for eye hath not seen, nor ear heard, neither have entered into the heart of man, the things which God hath prepared for them that love Him; and that all the difficulty arises from the fact that we have underbelieved and undertrusted.

I want, therefore, to show as best I can the grounds there are in the religion of the Lord Jesus Christ for that deep and lasting peace and comfort of soul, which nothing earthly can disturb, and which is declared to be the portion of those who embrace it. And I want further to tell, if this is indeed our rightful portion, how we are to avail ourselves of it, and what are the things that hinder. There is God's part in the matter, and there is man's part, and we must look carefully at both.

A wild young fellow, who was brought to the Lord at a mission meeting, and who became a rejoicing Christian and lived an exemplary life afterward, was asked by someone what he did to get converted. "Oh," he said, "I did my part, and the Lord did His."

"But what was your part," asked the inquirer, "and what was the Lord's part?"

"My part," was the prompt reply, "was to run away, and the Lord's part was to run after me until He caught me." A most significant answer; but how few can understand it!

God's part is always to run after us. Christ came to seek and to save that which is lost. "What man of you," He says, "having a hundred sheep, if he lose one of them, doth not leave the ninety and nine in the wilderness, and go after that which is lost until he find it? And when he hath found it, he layeth it on his shoulders rejoicing." This is always the divine part; but in our foolishness we do not understand it, but think that the Lord is the one who is lost, and that our part is to seek and find Him. The very expressions we use show this. We urge sinners to "seek the Lord," and we talk about having "found" Him. "Have you found the Saviour?" asked a too zealous mission worker of a happy, trusting little girl.

With a look of amazement, she replied in a tone of wonder, "Why, I did not know the Saviour was lost!"

It is our ignorance of God that does it all. Because we do not know Him, we naturally get all sorts of wrong ideas about Him. We think He is an angry Judge who is on the watch for our slightest faults, or a harsh Taskmaster determined to exact from us the uttermost service, or a self-absorbed Deity demanding His full measure of honor and glory, or a far-off Sovereign concerned only with His own affairs and indifferent to our welfare. Who can wonder that such a God can neither be loved nor trusted? And who could expect Christians, with such ideas concerning Him, to be anything but full of discomfort and misery?

But I can assert boldly, and without fear of contradiction, that it is impossible for anyone who really knows God to have such uncomfortable thoughts about Him. Plenty of outward discomforts there may be, and many earthly sorrows and trials, but through them all the soul that knows God cannot but dwell inwardly in a fortress of perfect peace. "Who so hearkeneth unto me," He says, "shall dwell safely; and shall be quiet from fear of evil." And this is a statement that no one dare question. If we would really hearken unto God, which means not only hearing Him, but believing what we hear, we could not fail to know that, just because He is God, He cannot do other than care for us as He cares for the apple of His eye; and that all that tender love and divine wisdom can do for our welfare, must be and will be unfailingly done. Not a single loophole for worry or fear is left to the soul that knows God.

"Ah, yes," you say, "but how am I to get to know Him. Other people seem to have some kind of inward revelation that makes them know Him, but I never do; and no matter how much I pray, everything seems dark to me. I want to know God, but I do not see how to manage it."

Your trouble is that you have got a wrong idea of what knowing God is, or at least the kind of knowing I mean. For I do not mean any mystical interior revelations of any kind. Such revelations are delightful when you can have them, but they are not always at your command, and they are often variable and uncertain. The kind of knowing I mean is just the plain matter-of-fact knowledge of God's nature and character that comes to us by believing what is revealed to us in the Bible concerning Him. The apostle John at the close of his Gospel says, regarding the things he had been recording: "And many other signs truly did Jesus in the presence of His disciples which are not written in this book: but these are written that ye might believe that Jesus is the Christ, the Son of God; and that, believing, ye might have life through his name." It is believing the thing that is written, not the thing that is inwardly revealed, that is to give life; and the kind of knowing I mean is the knowing that comes from believing the things that are written.

I mean, to be practical, that when I read in the Bible that God is love, I am to believe it, just because "it is written," and not because I have had any inward revelation that is true; and when the Bible says that He cares for us as He cares for the lilies of the field and the birds of the air, and that the very hairs of our head are all numbered, I am to believe it, just because it is written, no matter whether I have any inward revelation of it or not.

It is of vital importance for us to understand that the Bible is a statement, not of theories, but of actual facts; and that things are not true because they are in the Bible, but they are only in the Bible because they are true. A little boy, who had been studying at school about the discovery of America, said to his father one day, "Father, if I had been Columbus I would not have taken all that trouble to discover America."

"Why, what would you have done?" asked the father.

"Oh," replied the little boy, "I would have just gone to the map and found it." This little boy did not understand that maps are only pictures of already known places, and that America did not exist because it was on the map, but it could not be on the map until it was already known to exist. And similarly with the Bible. It is, like the map, a simple statement of facts; so that when it tells us that God loves us, it is only telling us something that is a fact, and that would not be in the Bible if it had not been already known to be a fact.

It was a great discovery to me when I grasped this idea. It seemed to take all uncertainty and all speculation out of the revelation given us in the Bible of the salvation of the Lord Jesus Christ, and to make all that is written concerning Him to be simply a statement of incontrovertible facts. And facts we can believe, and what is more, we do believe them as soon as we see that they are facts. Inward revelations we cannot manage, but anyone in his senses can believe the thing that is written. And although this may seem very dry and bare to start with, it will, if steadfastly persevered in, result in very blessed inward revelations, and will sooner or later lead us out into such a knowledge of God as will transform our lives. This kind of knowing brings us convictions; and to my mind convictions are far superior to any inward revelations, delightful as these last are. An inward revelation may be upset by the state of one's health, or by many other upsetting things, but a conviction is permanent. Once convince a man that two and two make four, and no amount of dyspepsia, or liver complaint, or east winds, or anything else, but actual lunacy, can upset his conviction. He knows it just as well when he has an attack of dyspepsia as he does when his digestion is in good working order. Convictions come from knowledge, and no amount of good feelings or bad feelings, of good health or ill health, can alter knowledge.

It is to try to help my readers to come to a knowledge of God in the plain matter-of-fact sort of way of which I have spoken, and to the convictions which result from this knowledge, that this book is written. I shall first try to show what God is, not theologically, nor doctrinally, but simply what He is in actual, practical reality, as the God and Father of each one of us. And I shall also point out some of the things that seem to me the principal hindrances to becoming really acquainted with Him.

I am so absolutely certain that coming to know Him as He really is will bring unfailing comfort and peace to every troubled heart that I long unspeakably to help everyone within my reach to this knowledge. One of Job's friends said, in his arguments against Job's bitter complaints, "Acquaint now thyself with God, and be at peace"; and our Lord in His last recorded prayer said: "This is life eternal, that they might know thee, the only true God, and Jesus Christ whom thou has sent." It is not a question of acquaintance with ourselves, or of knowing what we are, or what we do, or what we feel; it is simply and only a question of becoming acquainted with God, and getting to know what He is, and what He does, and what He feels. Comfort and peace never come from anything we know about ourselves, but only and always from what we know about Him.

We may spend our days in what we call our religious duties, and we may fill our devotions with fervor, and still may be miserable. Nothing can set our hearts at rest but a real acquaintance with God; for, after all, everything in our salvation must depend upon Him in the last instance; and, according as He is worthy or not of our confidence, so must necessarily be our comfort. If we were planning to take a dangerous voyage, our first question would be as to the sort of captain we were to have. Our common sense would tell us that if the captain were untrustworthy, no amount of trustworthiness on our part would make the voyage safe; and it would be his character and not our own that would be the thing of paramount importance to us.

If I can only say this often enough and in enough different ways to bring conviction to some troubled hearts, and lift them out of their sad and uncomfortable religious lives into the kingdom of love, and joy, and peace, which is their undisputed inheritance, I shall feel that my object in writing this book has been accomplished. And I shall be able to say, Lord, now lettest Thou Thy servant depart in peace, for mine eyes have seen Thy salvation; and my pen has tried to tell it.

It must, however, be clearly understood that my book does not propose to touch on the critical or the theological aspects of our religion. It does not undertake to deal with any questions concerning the authenticity of the Bible. Other and far abler minds can deal with these matters. My book is written for people, who, like myself, profess to believe in the Lord Jesus Christ, and who accept the Bible simply as the revelation of Him.

Putting aside all critical questions, therefore, I seek only to tell such believers of what seems to me the necessary result of their belief, and how they can personally realize this result.

Mistakes in the telling there may be, and for these I ask the charity of my readers. But the thing I want to say, and to say in such a way that no one can fail to understand it, is not a mistake; and that thing is this, that our religious lives ought to be full of joy, and peace, and comfort, and that, if we become better acquainted with God, they will be.

# Chapter Two - What is His Name?

"And Moses said unto God, Behold, when I come unto the children of Israel, and shall say unto them, The God of your fathers hath sent me unto you; and they shall say to me, What is his name? What shall I say unto them?"

The vital question of all ages and of every human heart is here expressed, "What is his name?"

The whole fate of humanity hangs on the answer to this question.

As we know, the condition of a country depends upon the character of its rulers. The state of an army depends upon the officers who command it. And the more absolute the government, the more is this necessarily the case.

We can see how it must be, therefore, that everything in a universe will depend upon the sort of creator and ruler who has brought that universe into existence, and that the whole welfare of the human beings who have been placed there is of necessity bound up with the character of their Creator. If the God who created us is a good God, then everything must of necessity be all right for us, since a good God cannot ordain any but good things. But if He is a bad God, or a careless God, or an unkind God, then we cannot be sure that anything is right, and can have no peace or comfort anywhere.

The true ground for peace and comfort is only to be found in the sort of God we have. Therefore, we need first of all to find out what is His name, or, in other words, what is His character—in short, what sort of a God He is.

In Bible language name always means character. Names are not given arbitrarily there, as with us, but are always given with reference to the character or work of the person named. Creden in his Concordance says that the names of God signify that which He really is, and are used throughout the Bible to express His attributes, and His purposes, His glory, His grace, His mercy, and His love, His wisdom, and power, and goodness. A careful study of His names will make this plain.

When, therefore, the children of Israel asked, "What is his name?" they meant, "Who and what is this God of whom you speak? What is His character; what are His attributes; what does He do? In short, what sort of a being is He?"

The psalmist says, "They that know thy name will put their trust in thee: for thou, Lord, hast not forsaken them that seek thee." And again he says, "The name of the

Lord is a strong tower, the righteous runneth into it and is safe." "They that know thy name will put their trust in thee." They cannot do anything else, because in knowing His name they know His character and His nature, that He is a God whom it is safe to trust to the uttermost. And there can be no doubt that a large part of the unrest and discomfort in so many Christian hearts comes simply from the fact that they do not yet know His name.

"Some trust in chariots and some in horses: but we will remember the name of the Lord our God. They are brought down and are fallen, but we are risen and stand upright." In all that we read concerning Israel of old we find this constant refrain, that all they were and all they had depended upon the fact that their God was the Lord. "Blessed is the nation whose God is the Lord; and the people whom he hath chosen for his own inheritance." "O Lord, there is none like thee, neither is there any God beside thee, according to all that we have heard with our ears. And what one nation in the earth is like thy people: to make thee a name of greatness and terribleness, by driving out nations from before thy people, whom thou hast redeemed out of Egypt? For thy people Israel didst thou make thine own people forever, and thou, Lord, becamest their God." "Happy is that people that is in the Lord."

Blessed is that nation, happy is that people whose God is the Lord! All the blessing and happiness of Israel arose from the fact that their God was the Lord. Nothing else was of sufficient importance to be mentioned in the recapitulation of their advantages. The fact that their God was the Lord Jehovah was enough to account for every good thing they possessed.

The question of all questions for each one of us, therefore, is this one, "What is his name?" To the Israelites God Himself answered this question. And God said unto Moses, "I am that I am"; and He said, "Thus shalt thou say unto the children of Israel, I Am hath sent me unto you." And God said, moreover, unto Moses: "Thus shalt thou say unto the children of Israel, the Lord God of your fathers, the God of Abraham, the God of Isaac, and the God of Jacob hath sent me unto you; this is my name forever, and this is my memorial unto all generations."

In the Gospel of John Christ adopts this name of "I am" as His own. When the Jews were questioning Him as to His authority, He said unto them: "Verily, verily, I say unto you, before Abraham was I am." And in the Book of Revelation He again declares: "I am Alpha and Omega, the beginning and the ending, saith the Lord, which is, and which was, and which is to come, the Almighty."

These simple words, I am, express therefore eternity and unchangeableness of existence, which is the very first element necessary in a God who is to be depended upon. No dependence could be placed by any one of us upon a changeable God. He must be the same yesterday, today, and forever, if we are to have any peace or comfort.

But is this all His name implies, simply "I am"? I am what?—we ask. What does this "I am" include?

I believe it includes everything the human heart longs for and needs. This unfinished name of God seems to me like a blank check signed by a rich friend given to us to be filled in with whatever sum we may desire. The whole Bible tells us what it means.

Every attribute of God, every revelation of His character, every proof of His undying love, every declaration of His watchful care, every assertion of His purposes of tender mercy, every manifestation of His loving kindness—all are the filling out of this unfinished "I am."

God tells us through all the pages of His Book what He is. "I am," He says, "all that my people need": "I am their strength"; "I am their wisdom"; "I am their righteousness"; "I am their peace"; "I am their salvation"; "I am their life"; "I am their all in all."

This apparently unfinished name, therefore, is the most comforting name the heart of man could devise, because it allows us to add to it, without any limitation, whatever we feel the need of, and even "exceeding abundantly" beyond all that we can ask or think.

But if our hearts are full of our own wretched "I ams" we will have no ears to hear His glorious, soul-satisfying "I am." We say, "Alas, I am such a poor weak creature," or "I am so foolish," or "I am so good-for-nothing," or "I am so helpless"; and we give these pitiful "I ams" of ours as the reason of the wretchedness and discomfort of our religious lives, and even feel that we are very much to be pitied that things are so hard for us. While all the time we entirely ignore the blank check of God's magnificent "I am," which authorizes us to draw upon Him for an abundant supply for every need.

If you are an uncomfortable Christian, then the only thing to give you a thoroughly comfortable religious life is to know God. The psalmist says that they that know God's name will put their trust in Him, and it is, I am convinced, impossible for anyone really to know Him and not to trust Him. A trustworthy person commands trust; not in the sense of ordering people to trust him, but by irresistibly winning their trust by his trustworthiness.

What our Lord declares is eternally true, "I, if I be lifted up, will draw all men unto me." When once you know Him, Christ is absolutely irresistible. You can no more help trusting Him than you can help breathing. And could the whole world but know Him as He is, the whole world, sinners and all, would fall at His feet in adoring worship. They simply could not help it. His surpassing loveliness would carry all before it.

How then can we become acquainted with God?

There are two things necessary: first, God must reveal Himself; and second, we must accept His revelation and believe what He reveals.

The apostle John tells us that "no man hath seen God at any time," but "the only begotten Son which is in the bosom of the Father, he hath declared him." Christ, then, is the revelation of God. We have none of us seen God, and we never can see Him in this present stage of our existence, for we have not the faculties that would make it possible. But He has incarnated Himself in Christ, and we can see Christ, since He was a man like one of us.

A man, who should want to talk with ants, might stand over an anthill and harangue for a whole day, and not one word would reach the ears of the ants. They would run to and fro utterly unconscious of his presence. As far as we know, ants have no faculties by which they can receive human communications. But if a man could incarnate himself in the body of an ant, and could go about among them, living an ant's life and speaking the ants' language, he would make himself intelligible to them at once. Incarnation is always necessary when a higher form of life would communicate with a lower.

Christ revealed God by what He was, by what He did, and by what He said. From the cradle to the grave, every moment of His life was a revelation of God. We must go to Him then for our knowledge of God, and we must refuse to believe anything concerning God that is not revealed to us in Christ. All other revelations are partial, and therefore not wholly true. Only in Christ do we see God as He is; for Christ is declared to be the "express image" of God.

Just what God would have said and done under the circumstances, that Christ said and did. "I do nothing of myself," was His continual assertion. "I say nothing of myself; the Father that dwelleth in me he doeth the works"; "I and my Father are one"; "He that seeth me seeth my Father".

Words could not tell us more plainly than the Bible tells us that in order to know God we have only to look at Christ; we have only to "receive the testimony" of Christ.

Over and over we are assured that God and Christ are one. When the Jews came to Christ, as He was walking in the porch of Solomon's Temple, and asked Him to tell them plainly who He was, He answered, "I and my Father are one." And to His disciples, at His last supper with them, He said, in answer to their questions: "If ye had known me, ye should have known my Father also, and from henceforth ye know him and have seen him." But Philip could not understand this, and said, "Lord, show us the Father, and it sufficeth us." And then Jesus repeated His former statement even more strongly: "Have I been so long time with you, and yet hast thou not known me Philip? He that hath seen me hath seen the Father; and how sayest thou then, Show us the Father?"

Nothing is more emphatically stated in the New Testament than this fact, that we are to behold the "light of the knowledge of the glory of God in the face of Jesus Christ," and that we can behold it fully nowhere else.

If we would know then the length, and breadth, and height, and depth of what God meant when He gave to Moses that apparently unfinished name of "I am," we shall find it revealed in Christ. He and He alone is the translation of God. He and He alone is the image of the invisible God.

It is evident, therefore, that we must never accept any conception of God that is contrary to what we see in Christ, and must utterly reject any view of His character or of His acts, or any statement of His relations with us as human beings, no matter how strongly upheld, which is at variance with what Christ has revealed.

We are all aware that the Old Testament revelation of God seems sometimes to contradict the revelation in Christ, and the question arises as to which we are to receive as the truest. In view of the fact that God Himself tells us that in these last days He has spoken to us by His Son, who is the "brightness of his glory and the express image of his person," we may not dare reject Christ's testimony, but must look upon the Old Testament revelation, where it differs from the revelation in Christ, as partial and imperfect; and must accept as a true setting forth of God only that which we find in Christ. Christ alone tells us the true and genuine name of God. In His last wonderful prayer He says: "I have manifested thy name unto the men whom thou gavest me out of the world, and they have known that all things whatsoever thou hast given me are of thee, for I have given unto them the words which thou gavest me; and they have received them, and have known surely that I came out from thee, and they have believed that thou didst send me."

Could we ask for greater authority than this?

In the whole life of Christ nothing is plainer or more emphatic than the fact that He claimed continually to be a full and complete manifestation of God. "The words that I speak unto you," He says, "I speak not of myself; but the Father that dwelleth in me, he doeth the works." Over and over He asserts that He says only what the Father tells Him to say. "I speak to the world those things which I have heard of him." "I do nothing of myself, but as my Father hath taught me I speak these things."

The apostle declares most emphatically that it "pleased the Father" that in Christ should "dwell all the fullness of the Godhead bodily." And although we may not understand all that this means theologically, we at least cannot fail to see that if we want to know God, we need only to become acquainted with Christ's ways and Christ's character in order to become acquainted with God's ways and God's character. "He that hath seen me," He says, "hath seen the Father." And again He declares that "neither knoweth any man the Father save the son, and he to whomsoever the Son will reveal him." This settles it beyond the possibility of cavil. We may, and we do, have all sorts of thoughts of God, we may conjecture this or imagine that, but we are wasting our energies in it all. We simply cannot know, no man can, except through the revelation of Christ.

We may know a good many things about Him, but that is very different from knowing Him Himself, as He really is in nature and character. Other witnesses have told us of His visible acts, but from these we get often very wrong impressions of His true character. No other witness but Christ can tell us of the real secrets of God's bosom, for of none other can it be said, as it is of Him, that "the only begotten Son who is in the bosom of the Father, he hath declared him." It will make all the difference between comfort and discomfort in our Christian lives, whether or not we believe this to be a fact. If we do believe it to be a fact, then the stern Judge and hard Taskmaster whom we have feared, even while we tried to follow Him, and whose service we have found so irksome and so full of discomfort, will disappear; and His place will be taken by the God of love who is revealed to us in "the face of Jesus Christ," the God who cares for us as He cares for the sparrows, and for the flowers of the field, and who tells us that He numbers even the hairs of our head.

No human being could be afraid of a God like this.

If we have been accustomed, therefore, to approach God with any mistrust of the kindness of His feelings toward us; if our religious life has been poisoned by fear; if unworthy thoughts of His character and will have filled our hearts with suspicions of His goodness; if we have pictured Him as an unjust deposit of a self-seeking tyrant; if, in short, we have imagined Him in any way other than that which has been revealed to us in "the face of Jesus Christ," we must go back in all simplicity of heart to the records of that lovely life, lived in human guise among men, and must bring our conceptions of God into perfect accord with the character and ways of Him who declares that He came to manifest the name of God to men.

In reply then to the question, "What is His name?" I have only this one thing to say, Ask Christ. We are told He was "God manifest in the flesh," and that whoever sees Him sees the God who sent Him; therefore it is perfectly plain that, if we want to know the name, we have only to read the manifestation. And this means simply that we must study the life, and words, and ways of Christ, and must say to ourselves, he that seeth Christ seeth God, and what Christ was on earth that God is in Heaven. All the darkness that enshrouds the character of God will vanish if we will but accept the light Christ has shed on the matter, and believe the "manifestation of His name" that Christ has given us, and will utterly refuse to believe anything else.

When Nicodemus came to Jesus by night to ask Him how the things He was saying could possibly be true, Jesus told him that, whether he understood them or not, they still were true, and said with greatest emphasis: "Verily, verily, I say unto thee, we speak that we do know, and testify that we have seen." No one who believes in Christ at all can doubt that He knew God; and no one can question whether or not we ought to receive His testimony. He has assured us over and over again that He knew what He was talking about, and that what He said was to be received as the absolute truth, because He had come down from Heaven, and therefore knew about heavenly things.

We none of us would dare openly to question the truth of this; and yet practically a great many of God's children utterly ignore Christ's testimony and choose instead to listen to the testimony of their own doubting hearts, which tells them it is impossible that God could be as loving in His care for us, or as tender toward our weakness and foolishness, or as ready to forgive our sins, as Christ has revealed Him to be. And yet I must repeat again and again, at the risk of being accused of useless repetition, what so few people seem to realize, that if there is one thing taught in the Bible more plainly than any other, it is that the name, or, in other words, the character of His Father which Christ gave, must be His real name and character. He declares of Himself over and over that He was a living manifestation of the Father; and in all He said and did He assures us that He was simply saying and doing that which the Father would have said and done had he acted directly out of Heaven, and from off His heavenly throne.

In the face of such unqualified assertions as these out of the lips of our Lord Himself, it becomes, not only our privilege, but our bounded duty to cast out of our conception of God every element that could in any way conflict with the blessed life and character and teaching of Christ. If we would know the real name of God, we must accept the name Christ has revealed to us, and must listen to no other.

Whatever characteristics then we see in Christ, these are the filling out of the "I am" of God. As we look at the life of Christ and listen to His words, we can hear God saying, "I am rest for the weary; I am peace for the storm-tossed; I am strength for the strengthless; I am wisdom for the foolish; I am righteousness for the sinful; I am all that the neediest soul on earth can want; I am exceeding abundantly, beyond all you can ask or think, or blessing, and help, and care."

But here the doubter may say, "Ah yes, this is no doubt all true, but how can I get hold of it? I am such a poor, unworthy creature that I dare not believe such a fullness of grace can belong to me."

How can you get hold of it, you ask. You cannot get hold of it at all, but you can let it get hold of you. It is a piece of magnificent good news declared to you in the Bible; and you only need do with it exactly what you do when any earthly good news is told you by a reliable earthly source. If the speaker is trustworthy, you believe what he says, and act in accordance. And you must do the same here. If Christ is trustworthy when He tells you that He is the manifestation of God, you must believe what He says, and act accordingly.

You must take your stand on His trustworthiness. You must say to yourself, and to your friends if need be, "I am going to believe what Christ says about God. No matter what the seemings may be, nor what my own thoughts and feelings are, nor what anybody else may say, I know that what Christ says about God must be true, for He knew, and nobody else does, and I am going to believe Him right straight through, come what may. He says that He was one with God, so all that He was God is, and I will never be frightened of God any more. I will never again let myself think of Him as a stern Lawgiver who is angry with me because of my sins, nor as a hard Taskmaster who demands from me impossible tasks, nor as a far-off unapproachable Deity, who is wrapped up in His own glory, and is indifferent to my sorrows and my fears. All such ideas of God have become impossible, now that I know that Christ was the true manifestation of God."

If we will take our stand on this one fact, that Christ and God are one, with an intelligent comprehension of what it involves, and will refuse definitely and unwaveringly to cherish any thought of God that is at variance with what Christ has revealed, life will be transformed for us.

We may often have to set our faces like a flint to hold steadfastly here; for our old doubts and fears will be sure to come back and demand admittance; but we must turn our backs on them resolutely, and must declare that now at last we know the name, or in other words, the character of our God, and know that such things would be impossible to Him; and that therefore we simply refuse point-blank to listen for a moment to any such libels on His character or His ways.

It is unthinkable to suppose that when God told Moses His name was "I am," He could have meant to say, "I am a stern Lawgiver," or "I am a hard Taskmaster," or "I am a God who is wrapped up in my own glory, and am indifferent to the sorrows or the fears of my people." If we should try to fill in the blank of His "I am" with such things as these, all the Christians the world over would be horrified. But do not the doubts and fears of some of these very Christians say exactly these things in secret every day of their lives?

May God grant that what we shall learn in our consideration of the names of God may make all such doubts and fears impossible to us from this time forth and forevermore.

*Jesus is God! Oh, could I now*
*But compass land and sea,*
*To teach and tell this single truth,*
*How happy I should be!*
*Oh, had I but an angel's voice,*
*I would proclaim so loud—*
*Jesus, the good, the beautiful,*
*Is the image of our God!*

# Chapter Three - The God of All Comfort

"Blessed be God, even the Father of our Lord Jesus Christ, the Father of mercies and the God of all comfort; who comforteth us in all our tribulations, that we may be able to comfort them which are in any trouble, by the comfort wherewith we ourselves are comforted of God."

Among all the names that reveal God, this, the "God of all comfort," seems to me one of the loveliest and the most absolutely comforting. The words all comfort admit of no limitation and no deductions; and one would suppose that, however full of discomforts the outward life of the followers of such a God might be, their inward religious life must necessarily be always and under all circumstances a comfortable life. But, as a fact, it often seems as if exactly the opposite were the case, and the religious lives of large numbers of the children of God are full, not of comfort, but of the utmost discomfort. This discomfort arises from anxiety as to their relationship to God, and doubts as to His love. They torment themselves with the thought that they are too good-for-nothing to be worthy of His care, and they suspect Him of being indifferent to their trials and of forsaking them in times of need. They are anxious and troubled about everything in their religious life, about their disposition and feelings, their indifference to the Bible, their want of fervency in prayer, their coldness of heart. They are tormented with unavailing regrets over their past, and with devouring anxieties for their future. They feel unworthy to enter God's presence, and dare not believe that they belong to Him. They can be happy and comfortable with their earthly friends, but they cannot be happy or comfortable with God. And although He declares Himself to be the God of all comfort, they continually complain that they cannot find comfort anywhere; and their sorrowful looks and the doleful tones of their voice show that they are speaking the truth.

Such Christians, although they profess to be the followers of the God of all comfort, spread gloom and discomfort around them wherever they go; and it is out of the question for them to hope that they can induce anyone else to believe that this beautiful name, by which He has announced Himself, is anything more than a pious phrase, which in reality means nothing at all. And the manifestly uncomfortable religious lives of so many Christians is, I am very much afraid, responsible for a large part of the unbelief of the world.

The apostle says that we are to be living epistles known and read of all men; and the question as to what men read in us is of far more vital importance to the spread of Christ's kingdom than we half the time realize. It is not what we say that tells, but what we are. It is easy enough to say a great many beautiful things about God being the God of all comfort; but unless we know what it is to be really and truly comforted ourselves, we might as well talk to the winds. People must read in our lives what they hear in our words, or all our preaching is worse than useless. It would be well for us to ask ourselves what they are reading in us. Is it comfort or discomfort that voices itself in our daily walk and life?

But at this point I may be asked what I mean by the comfort God gives. Is it a sort of pious grace, that may perhaps fit us for Heaven, but that is somehow unfit to bear the brunt of our everyday life with its trials and its pains? Or is it an honest and genuine comfort, as we understand comfort, that enfolds life's trials and pains in an all embracing peace?

With all my heart I believe it is the latter.

Comfort, whether human or divine, is pure and simple comfort, and is nothing else. We none of us care for pious phrases, we want realities; and the reality of being comforted and comfortable seems to me almost more delightful than any other thing in life. We all know what it is. When as little children we have cuddled up into our mother's lap after a fall or a misfortune, and have felt her dear arms around us, and her soft kisses on our hair, we have had comfort. When, as grown-up people, after a hard day's work, we have put on our slippers and seated ourselves by the fire, in an easy chair with a book, we have had comfort. When, after a painful illness, we have begun to recover, and have been able to stretch our limbs and open our eyes without pain, we have had comfort. When someone whom we dearly love has been ill almost unto death, and has been restored to us in health again, we have had comfort. A thousand times in our lives probably, have we said, with a sigh of relief, as a toil over or burdens laid down, "Well, this is comfortable," and in that word comfortable there has been comprised more a rest, and relief, and satisfaction, and pleasure, than any other word in the English language could possibly be made to express. We cannot fail, therefore, to understand the meaning of this name of God, the "God of all comfort."

But alas, we have failed to believe it. It has seemed to us too good to be true. The joy and delight of it, if it were really a fact, have been more than our poor suspicious natures could take in. We may venture to hope sometimes that little scraps of comfort may be vouchsafed to us; but we have run away frightened at the thought of the "all comfort" that is ours in the salvation of the Lord Jesus Christ.

And yet what more could He have said about it than He has said: "As one whom his mother comforteth, so will I comfort you; and ye shall be comforted." Notice the as and so in this passage: "As one whom his mother comforteth, so will I comfort you." It is real comforting that is meant here; the sort of comforting that a child feels when it is "dandled on its mother's knees, and borne on her sides"; and yet how many of us have really believed that God's comforting is actually as tender and true as a mother's comforting, or even half or quarter so real. Instead of thinking of ourselves as being "dandled" on His knees, and hugged to His heart, as mothers hug, have we not rather been inclined to look upon Him as a stern, unbending Judge, holding us at a distance, and demanding our respectful homage, and critical of our slightest faults? Is it any wonder that our religion, instead of making us comfortable, has made us thoroughly uncomfortable? Who could help being uncomfortable in the presence of such a Judge?

But I rejoice to say that that stern Judge is not there. He does not exist. The God who does exist is a God who is like a mother, a God who says to us as plainly as words can say it, "As one whom his mother comforteth, so will I comfort you."

Over and over again He declares this. "I, even I, am he that comforteth you," He says to the poor, frightened children of Israel. And then He reproaches them with not being comforted. "Why," He says, "should you let anything make you afraid when here is the Lord, your Maker, ready and longing to comfort you. You have feared continually every day the 'fury of the oppressor,' and have forgotten me who have stretched forth the heavens and laid the foundations of the earth? Where is the fury of the oppressor when I am by?"

The God who exists is the God and the Father of our Lord Jesus Christ, the God who so loved the world that He sent His Son, not to judge the world, but to save it. He is the God who "anointed" the Lord Jesus Christ to bind up the brokenhearted, and to proclaim liberty to the captives, and the opening of the prison to them that are bound, and to comfort all that mourn. Please notice that all. Not a few select ones only, but all. Every captive of sin, every prisoner in infirmity, every mourning heart throughout the whole world must be included in this "all." It would not be "all" if there should be a single one left out, no matter how insignificant, or unworthy, or even how feeble-minded that one might be. I have always been thankful that the feeble-minded are especially mentioned by Paul in his exhortations to the Thessalonian Christians, when he is urging them to comfort one another. In effect he says, Do not scold the feeble-minded, but comfort them. The very ones who need comfort most are the ones that our God, who is like a mother, wants to comfort—not the strong-minded ones, but the feeble-minded.

For this is the glory of a religion of love. And this is the glory of the religion of the Lord Jesus Christ. He was anointed to comfort "all that mourn." The "God of all comfort" sent His Son to be the comforter of a mourning world. And all through His life on earth He fulfilled His divine mission. When His disciples asked Him to call down fire from Heaven to consume some people who refused to receive Him, He turned and rebuked them, and said: "Ye know not what manner of spirit ye are of. For the Son of man is not come to destroy men's lives but to save them." He received sinners and ate with them. He welcomed Mary Magdalene when all men turned from her. He refused even to condemn the woman who was taken in the very act of sin, but said to the scribes and Pharisees who had brought her before Him, "He that is without sin among you, let him first cast a stone at her"; and when, convicted by their own consciences, they all went out one by one without condemning her, He said to her, "Neither do I condemn thee: go, and sin no more." Always and everywhere He was on the side of sinners. That was what He was for. He came to save sinners. He had no other mission.

Two little girls were talking about God, and one said, "I know God does not love me. He could not care for such a teeny, tiny little girl as I am."

"Dear me, sis," said the other little girl, "don't you know that that is just what God is for—to take care of teeny, tiny little girls who can't take care of themselves, just like us?"

"Is He?" said the first little girl. "I did not know that. Then I don't need to worry any more, do I?"

If any troubled doubting heart, any heart that is fearing continually every day some form or other of evil should read these lines, let me tell you again in trumpet tones that this is just what the Lord Jesus Christ is for—to care for and comfort all who mourn. "All," remember, every single one, even you yourself, for it would not be "all" if you were left out. You may be so cast down that you can hardly lift up your head, but the apostle tells us that He is the "God that comforteth those that are cast down"; the comforting of Christ. All who mourn, all who are cast down—I love to think of such a mission of comfort in a world of mourning like ours; and I long to see every cast down and sorrowing heart comforted with this comforting of God.

And our Comforter is not far off in Heaven where we cannot find Him. He is close at hand. He abides with us. When Christ was going away from this earth, He told His disciples that He would not leave them comfortless, but would send "another Comforter" who would abide with them forever. This Comforter, He said, would teach them all things, and would bring all things to their remembrance. And then He declared, as though it were the necessary result of the coming of this divine Comforter: "Peace I leave with you, my peace I give unto you; not as the world giveth, give I unto you. Let not your heart [therefore] be troubled, neither let it be afraid." Oh, how can we, in the face of these tender and loving words, go about with troubled and frightened hearts.

"Comforter"—what a word of bliss, if we only could realize it. Let us repeat it over and over to ourselves, until its meaning sinks into the very depths of our being. And an "abiding" Comforter, too, not one who comes and goes, and is never on hand when most needed, but one who is always present, and always ready to give us "joy for mourning, and the garment of praise for the spirit of heaviness."

The very words abiding Comforter are an amazing revelation. Try to comprehend them. If we can have a human comforter to stay with us for only a few days when we are in trouble, we think ourselves fortunate; but here is a divine Comforter who is always staying with us, and whose power to comfort is infinite. Never, never ought we for a single minute to be without comfort; never for a single minute ought we to be uncomfortable.

I have often wondered whether those early disciples realized at all what this glorious legacy of a Comforter meant. I am very sure the majority of the disciples of Christ now do not. If they did, there could not possibly be so many uncomfortable Christians about.

But you may ask whether this divine Comforter does not sometimes reprove us for our sins, and whether we can get any comfort out of this. In my opinion this is exactly one of the places where the comfort comes in. For what sort of creatures should we be if we had no divine Teacher always at hand to show us our faults and awaken in us a desire to get rid of them?

If I am walking along the street with a very disfiguring hole in the back of my dress, of which I am in ignorance, it is certainly a very great comfort to me to have a kind friend who will tell me of it. And similarly it is indeed a comfort to know that there is always abiding with me a divine, all-seeing Comforter, who will reprove me for all my faults, and will not let me go on in a fatal unconsciousness of them. Emerson says it is far more to a man's interest that he should see his own faults than that anyone else should see them, and a moment's thought will convince us that this is true, and will make us thankful for the Comforter who reveals them to us.

I remember vividly the comfort it used to be to me, when I was young, to have a sister who always knew what was the right and proper thing to do, and who, when we went out together, always kept me in order. I never felt any anxiety or responsibility about myself if she was by, for I knew she would keep a strict watch over me, and nudge me or whisper to me if I was making any mistakes. I was always made comfortable, and not uncomfortable, by her presence. But when it chanced that I went anywhere alone, then I would indeed feel uncomfortable, for then there was no one near to keep me straight.

The declaration is that He "comforts all our waste places"; and He does this by revealing them to us, and at the same time showing us how He can make our "wildernesses like Eden," and our "deserts like the garden of the Lord."

You may object, perhaps, because you are not worthy of His comforts. I do not suppose you are. No one ever is. But you need His comforting, and because you are not worthy you need it all the more. Christ came into the world to save sinners, not good people, and your unworthiness is your greatest claim for His salvation.

In the same passage in Isaiah in which He tells us that He has seen our ways and was "wroth" with us, He assures us that He will heal us and restore comforts to us. It is just because He is wroth with us (wroth in the sense in which love is always wroth with any fault in those it loves), that therefore He "restores comforts" to us. And He does it by revealing our sin and healing it.

The avenue to the comfortings of the divine Comforter lies through the need of comfort. And this explains to me better than anything else the reason why the Lord so often allows sorrow and trial to be our portion. "Therefore, behold, I will allure her, and bring her into the wilderness, and speak comfortably unto her." We find ourselves, it may be, in a "wilderness" of disappointment and of suffering, and we wonder why the God who loves us should have allowed it. But he knows that it is only in that very wilderness that we can hear and receive the "comfortable words" He has to pour out upon us. We must feel the need of comfort before we can listen to the words of comfort. And God knows that it is infinitely better and happier for us to need His comforts and receive them, than ever it could be not to need them and so be without them. The consolations of God mean the substituting of a far higher and better thing for what we lose to get them. The things we lose are earthly things, those He substitutes are heavenly. And who of us but would thankfully be "allured" by our God into any earthly wilderness, if only there we might find the unspeakable joys of union with Himself. Paul could say he "counted all things but loss" if he might but "win Christ"; and, if we have even the faintest glimpse of what winning Christ means, we will say so too.

But strangely enough, while it is easy for us when we are happy and do not need comforting, to believe that our God is the "God of all comfort," but as soon as we are in trouble and need it, it seems impossible to believe that there can be any comfort for us anywhere. It would almost seem as if, in our reading of the Bible, we had reversed its meaning, and made it say, not "Blessed are they that mourn, for they shall be comforted," but "Blessed are they that rejoice, for they, and they only, shall be comforted." It is very strange how often in our secret hearts we almost unconsciously alter the Bible words a little, and so make the meaning exactly opposite to what it actually is; or else we put in so many "ifs" and "buts" as to take the whole point out of what is said. Take for instance, those beautiful words, "God that comforteth those that are cast down," and ask ourselves whether we have never been tempted to make it read in our secret hearts, "God who forsaketh those who are cast down," or, "God who overlooks those who are cast down," or, "God who will comfort those who are cast down if they show themselves worthy of comfort"; and whether, consequently, instead of being comforted, we have not been plunged into misery and despair.

The psalmist tells us that God will "comfort us on every side," and what an all-embracing bit of comfort this is. "On every side," no aching spot to be left uncomforted. And yet, in times of special trial, how many Christians secretly read this as though it said, "God will comfort us on every side except just the side where our trials lie; on that side there is no comfort anywhere." But God says every side, and it is only unbelief on our part that leads us to make an exception of our special side.

It is with too many, alas, just as it was with Israel of old. On one side God said to Zion: "Sing, O heavens, and be joyful, O earth, and break forth into singing, O mountains; for the Lord hath comforted his people, and will have mercy upon his afflicted"; and on the other side Zion said, "The Lord hath forsaken me, and my Lord hath forgotten me." And then God's answer came in those wonderful words, full forever of comfort enough to meet the needs of all the sorrows of all humanity: "Forget thee! Can a mother forget? Yea, perhaps a mother may forget, but I cannot. I have even graven thee upon the palms of my hands, so that it is impossible for me to forget thee! Be comforted, then, and sing for you."

But you may ask how you are to get hold of this divine comfort. My answer is that you must take it. God's comfort is being continually and abundantly given, but unless you will accept it you cannot have it.

Divine comfort does not come to us in any mysterious or arbitrary way. It comes as the result of a divine method. The indwelling Comforter "brings to our remembrance" comforting things concerning our Lord, and, if we believe them, we are comforted by them. A text is brought to our remembrance, perhaps, or the verse of a hymn, or some thought concerning the love of Christ and His tender care for us. If we receive the suggestion in simple faith, we cannot help being comforted. But if we refuse to listen to the voice of our Comforter, and insist instead on listening to the voice of discouragement or despair, no comfort can by any possibility reach our souls.

It is very possible for even a mother to lavish in vain all her stores of motherly comfort on a weeping child. The child sits up stiff and sullen, and "refuses to be comforted." All her comforting words fall on unbelieving ears. For to be comforted by comforting words it is absolutely necessary for us to believe these words. God has spoken "comforting words" enough, one would think, to comfort a whole universe, and yet we see all around us unhappy Christians, and worried Christians, and gloomy Christians, into whose comfortless hearts not one of these comforting words seems to be allowed to enter. In fact, a great many Christians actually think it is wrong to be comforted. They feel too unworthy. And if any rays of comfort steal into their hearts, they sternly shut them out; and like Rachel and Jacob, and the psalmist, their souls "refuse to be comforted."

The apostle tells us that whatsoever things are written in the Scriptures are for our learning, in order that we "through patience and comfort of the Scriptures may have hope." But if we are to be comforted by the Scriptures, we must first believe them. Nothing that God has said can possibly comfort a person who does not believe it to be really true. When the captain of a vessel tells us that his vessel is safe, we must first believe him to be telling the truth, before we can feel comfortable on board that vessel. When the conductor on a railway tells us we are on the right train, before we can settle down comfortably in our seats, we must trust his word. This is all so self-evident that it might seem folly to call attention to it. But in religious matters it often happens that the self-evident truths are the very ones most easily overlooked; and I have actually known people who insisted on realizing God's comfort while still doubting His words of comfort; and who even thought they could not believe His comforting words at all, until they had first felt the comfort in their own souls! As well might the passenger on the railway insist on having a feeling of comfortable assurance that he is on the right train, before he could make up his mind to believe the word of the conductor. Always and in everything comfort must follow faith, and can never precede it.

In this matter of comfort it is exactly as it is in every other experience in the religious life. God says, "Believe, and then you can feel." We say, "Feel, and then we can believe." God's order is not arbitrary, it exists in the very nature of things; and in all earthly matters we recognize this, and are never so foolish as to expect to feel we have anything until we first believe that it is in our possession. I could not possibly feel glad that I had a fortune in the bank, unless I knew that it was really there. But in spiritual things we reverse God's order (which is the order of nature as well), and refuse to believe that we possess anything until we first feel as if we had it.

Let me illustrate. We are, let us suppose, overwhelmed with cares and anxieties. It often happens in this world. To comfort us in these circumstances the Lord assures us that we need not be anxious about anything, but may commit all our cares to Him, for He careth for us. We are all familiar with the passages where He tells us to "behold the fowls of the air," and to "consider the lilies of the field" and assures us that we are of much more value than they, and that, if He cares for them, He will much more care for us. One would think there was comfort enough here for every care or sorrow all the wide world over. To have God assume our cares and our burdens, and carry them for us; the Almighty God, the Creator of Heaven and earth, who can control everything, and foresee everything, and consequently can manage everything in the very best possible way, to have Him declare that He will undertake for us; what could possibly be a greater comfort? And yet how few people are really comforted by it. Why is this? Simply and only because they do not believe it. They are waiting to have an inward feeling that His words are true, before they will believe them. They look upon them as beautiful things for Him to say, and they wish they could believe them, but they do not think they can be true in their own special case, unless they can have an inward feeling that they are; and if they should speak out honestly, they would confess that, since they have no such inward feeling, they do not believe His words apply to them; and as a consequence they do not in the least expect Him actually to care for their affairs at all. "Oh, if I could only feel it was all true," we say; and God says, "Oh, if you would only believe it is all true!"

It is pure and simple unbelief that is at the bottom of all our lack of comfort, and absolutely nothing else. God comforts us on every side, but we simply do not believe His words of comfort.

The remedy for this is plain. If we want to be comforted, we must make up our minds to believe every single solitary word of comfort God has ever spoken; and we must refuse utterly to listen to any words of discomfort spoken by our own hearts, or by our circumstances. We must set our faces like a flint to believe, under each and every sorrow and trial, in the divine Comforter, and to accept and rejoice in His all-embracing comfort. I say, "set our faces like a flint," because, when everything around us seems out of sorts, it is not always easy to believe God's words of comfort. We must put our wills into this matter of being comforted, just as we have to put our wills into all other matters in our spiritual life. We must choose to be comforted.

It may seem impossible, when things look all wrong and uncared for, to believe that God really can be caring for us as a mother cares for her children; and, although we know perfectly well that He says He does care for us in just this tender and loving way, yet we say, "Oh, if I could only believe that, of course I should be comforted." Now here is just where our wills must come in. We must believe it. We must say to ourselves, "God says it, and it is true, and I am going to believe it, no matter how it looks." And then we must never suffer ourselves to doubt or question it again.

I do not hesitate to say that whoever will adopt this plan will come, sooner or later, into a state of abounding comfort.

The psalmist says, "In the multitude of my thoughts within me thy comforts delight my soul." But I am afraid that among the multitude of our thoughts within us there are far too often many more thoughts of our own discomforts than of God's comforts. We must think of His comforts if we are to be comforted by them. It might be a good exercise of soul for some of us to analyze our thoughts for a few days, and see how many thoughts we actually do give to God's comforts, compared with the number we give to our own discomforts. I think the result would amaze us!

One word I must add in conclusion. If any of my readers are preachers of the Gospel of our Lord Jesus Christ, I would like to ask them what they are commissioned to preach.

The true commission in my opinion is to be found in Isaiah 40:1,2: "Comfort ye, comfort ye my people, saith your God. Speak ye comfortably to Jerusalem, and cry unto her, that her warfare is accomplished, that her iniquity is pardoned; for she hath received of the Lord's hand double for all her sins." "Comfort ye my people" is the divine command; do not scold them. If it is the Gospel you feel called to preach, then see to it that you do really preach Christ's Gospel and not man's. Christ comforts, man scolds. Christ's Gospel is always good news, and never bad news. Man's gospel is generally a mixture of a little good news and a great deal of bad news; and even where it tries to be good news, it is so hampered with "ifs" and "buts," and with all sorts of man-made conditions, that it utterly fails to bring any lasting joy or comfort.

The only Gospel that, to my thinking, can rightly be called the Gospel is that one proclaimed by the angel to the frightened shepherds, who were in the field keeping watch over their flocks by night: "Fear not," said the angel, "for behold I bring you good tidings of great joy, which shall be to all people. For unto you is born this day in the city of David, a Saviour which is Christ the Lord."

Never were more comfortable words preached to any congregation. And if only all the preachers in all the pulpits would speak the same comfortable words to the people; and if all the congregations, who hear these words, would believe them, and would take the comfort of them, there would be no more uncomfortable Christians left anywhere. And over the whole land would be fulfilled the apostle's prayer for the Thessalonians: "Now our Lord Jesus Christ himself, and God, even our Father, which hath loved us and hath given us everlasting consolation and good hope through grace, comfort your hearts, and stablish you in every good word and work."

# Chapter Four - The Lord Our Shepherd

"The Lord is my shepherd, I shall not want."

Perhaps no aspect in which the Lord reveals Himself to us is fuller of genuine comfort than the aspect set forth in the Twenty-third Psalm, and in its corresponding passage in the tenth chapter of John.

The psalmist tells me that the Lord is my Shepherd, and the Lord Himself declares that He is the good Shepherd. Can we conceive of anything more comforting?

It is a very wonderful thing that the highest and grandest truths of the religion of the Lord Jesus Christ are so often shut up in the simplest and commonest texts in the Bible. Those texts with which we have been familiar from our childhood, which we learned in the nursery at our mother's knee, which were used by those who loved us to explain in the simplest possible way the love of our heavenly Father, and the reasons for our trusting Him—these very texts, I have discovered, contain in their simple statements the whole story.

I feel, therefore, that what we all need is just to get back into the nursery again, and take up our childish verses once more, and, while reading them with the intelligence of our grown-up years, to believe them with all our old childish faith.

Let me carry you back then with me, my dear reader, to the children's psalm, that one which is so universally taught to the little ones in the nursery and in the infant school. Do we not each one of us remember the Twenty-third Psalm, as long as we can remember anything, and can we not recall even now something of the joy and pride of our childish hearts when first we were able to repeat it without mistake? Since then we have always known it, and at this moment its words, perhaps, sound so old and familiar to some of you, that you cannot see what meaning they can convey.

But in truth they tell us the whole story of our religion in words of such wondrous depth of meaning that I very much doubt whether it has ever yet entered into the heart of any mortal man to conceive of the things they reveal.

Repeat these familiar words over to yourselves afresh: "The Lord is my shepherd, I shall not want."

Who is it that is your shepherd?

The Lord! Oh, my friends, what a wonderful announcement! The Lord God of Heaven and earth, the Almighty Creator of all things, He who holds the universe in His hand as though it were a very little thing, He is your Shepherd, and has charged Himself with the care and keeping of you, as a shepherd is charged with the care and keeping of his sheep.

If your hearts will only take in this thought, I can promise you that your religion will from henceforth be full of the profoundest comfort, and all your old uncomfortable religion will drop off forever, as the mist disappears in the blaze of the summer sun.

I had a vivid experience of this at one time in my Christian life. The Twenty-third Psalm had, of course, always been familiar to me from my nursery days, but it had never seemed to have any special meaning. Then came a critical moment in my life when I was sadly in need of comfort, but could see none anywhere. I could not at the moment lay my hands on my Bible, and I cast about in my mind for some passage of Scripture that would help me. Immediately there flashed into my mind the words, "The Lord is my shepherd, I shall not want." At first I turned from it almost with scorn. "Such a common text as that," I said to myself, "is not likely to do me any good"; and I tried hard to think of a more recherché one, but none would come; and at last it almost seemed as if there were no other text in the whole Bible. And finally I was reduced to saying "Well, if I cannot think of any other text, I must try to get what little good I can out of this one," and I began to repeat to myself over and over, "The Lord is my shepherd, I shall not want." Suddenly, as I did so, the words were divinely illuminated, and there poured out upon me such floods of comfort that I felt as if I could never have a trouble again.

The moment I could get hold of a Bible I turned over its leaves with eagerness to see whether it could possibly be true that such untold treasures of comfort were really and actually mine, and whether I might dare to let out my heart into the full enjoyment of them. And I did what I have often found great profit in doing, I built up a pyramid of declarations and promises concerning the Lord being our Shepherd that, once built, presented an immovable and indestructible front to all the winds and storms of doubt or trial that could assail it. And I became convinced, beyond a shadow of doubt, that the Lord really was my Shepherd, and that in giving Himself this name He assumed the duties belonging to the name, and really would be, what He declares Himself to be, a "good shepherd who giveth his life for his sheep."

He Himself draws the contrast between a good shepherd and a bad shepherd, when He follows up His announcement "I am the good shepherd," with the words, "But he that is an hireling and not the shepherd, whose own the sheep are not, seeth the wolf coming and leaveth the sheep and fleeth; and the wolf catcheth them and scattereth the sheep." And through the mouth of His prophets the Lord pours down a scathing condemnation upon all such faithless shepherds.

"And the Lord saith unto me," says the prophet Zechariah, "take unto thee yet the instruments of a foolish shepherd....Woe to the idle shepherd that leaveth the flock! The sword shall be upon his arm, and upon his right eye; his arm shall be clean dried up, and his right eye shall be utterly darkened."

Again the prophet Ezekiel says: "Thus saith the Lord God unto the shepherds: Woe be to the shepherds of Israel that do feed themselves! Should not the shepherds feed the flocks? ... The diseased have ye not strengthened, neither have ye healed that which was sick, neither have ye bound up that which was broken, neither have ye brought back that which was driven away, neither have ye sought that which was lost; but with force and with cruelty have ye ruled them ... Therefore, O ye shepherds, hear the word of the Lord: Thus saith the Lord God, Behold I am against the shepherds, and I will require my flock at their hand, and cause them to cease from feeding the flock."

Surely one would think that no Christian could ever accuse our divine Shepherd of being as faithless and unkind as those He thus condemns. And yet, if the secrets of some Christian hearts should be revealed, I fear that it would be found that, although they do not put it into words, and perhaps hardly know themselves that such are their feelings about Him, yet at the bottom they do really look upon Him as a faithless Shepherd.

What else can it mean when Christians complain that the Lord has forsaken them; that they cry to Him for spiritual food and He does not hear; that they are beset by enemies on every side and He does not deliver them; that when their souls find themselves in dark places He does not come to their rescue; that when they are weak He does not strengthen them; and when they are spiritually sick He does not heal them?

What are all these doubts and discouragements but secret accusations against our good Shepherds of the very things which He Himself so scathingly condemns?

A dear Christian, who had just discovered what it meant to have known that that was what He was called, but it meant nothing to me; and I believe I read the Twenty-third Psalm as though it was written, 'The Lord is the sheep, and I am the shepherd, and, if I do not keep a tight hold on Him, He will run away.' When dark days came I never for a moment thought that He would stick by me, and when my soul was starving and cried out for food, I never dreamed He would feed me. I see now that I never looked upon Him as a faithful Shepherd at all. But now all is different. I myself am not one bit better or stronger, but I have discovered that I have a good Shepherd, and that is all I need. I see now that it really is true that the Lord is my Shepherd, and that I shall not want."

Dear fellow Christian, I pray you to look this matter fairly in the face. Are you like the Christian I have quoted above? You have said, I know, hundreds of times, "The Lord is my shepherd," but have you ever really believed it to be an actual fact? Have you felt safe and happy and free from care, as a sheep must feel when under the care of a good shepherd, or have you felt yourself to be like a poor forlorn sheep without a shepherd, or with an unfaithful, inefficient shepherd, who does not supply your needs, and who leaves you in times of danger and darkness?

I beg of you to answer this question honestly in your own soul. Have you had a comfortable religious life or an uncomfortable one? If the latter has been your condition, how can you reconcile it with the statement that the Lord is your Shepherd, and therefore you shall not want? You say He is your Shepherd, and yet you complain that you do want. Who has made the mistake? You or the Lord?

But here, perhaps, you will meet me with the words, "Oh, no, I do not blame the Lord, but I am so weak and so foolish, and so ignorant, that I am not worthy of His care." But do you not know that sheep are always weak, and helpless, and silly; and that the very reason they are compelled to have a shepherd to care for them is just because they are so unable to take care of themselves? Their welfare and their safety, therefore, do not in the least depend upon their own strength, nor upon their own wisdom, nor upon anything in themselves, but wholly and entirely upon the care of their shepherd. And, if you are a sheep, your self also must depend altogether upon your Shepherd, and not at all upon yourself.

Let us imagine two flocks of sheep meeting at the end of the winter to compare their experiences—one flock fat and strong and in good condition, and the other poor and lean and diseased. Will the healthy flock boast of themselves, and say, "See what splendid care we have taken of ourselves, what good, strong, wise sheep we must be?" Surely not. Their boasting would all be about their shepherd. "See what a good shepherd we have had," they would say, "and how he has cared for us. Through all the storms of the winter he has protected us, and has defended us from every wild beast, and has always provided us with the best of food."

Or, on the other hand, would the poor, wretched, diseased sheep blame themselves and say, "Alas, what wicked sheep we must be, to be in such a poor condition!" No, they too would speak only of their shepherd, but how different would be their story! "Alas," they would say, "our shepherd was very different from yours! He fed himself, but he did not feed us. He did not strengthen us when we were weak, nor heal us when we were sick, nor bind us up when we were broken nor look for us when we were lost. It is true he stayed by us in clear and pleasant weather, when no enemies were nigh, but in times of danger or of storm, he forsook us and fled. Oh, that we had had a good shepherd like yours!"

We all understand this responsibility of the shepherd in the case of sheep; but the moment we transfer the figure to our religion, we at once shift all the responsibility off the Shepherd's shoulders, and lay it upon the sheep; and demand of the poor human sheep the wisdom, and care, and power to provide, that can only belong to the divine Shepherd and be met by Him; and of course the poor human sheep fail, and their religious lives become thoroughly uncomfortable, and even sometimes most miserable.

I freely confess there is a difference between sheep and ourselves in this, that they have neither the intelligence nor the power to withdraw themselves from the care of their shepherd, while we have. We cannot imagine one of them saying, "Oh, yes, we have a good shepherd who says he will take care of us, but then we do not feel worthy of his care, and therefore we are afraid to trust him. He says he has provided for us green pastures and a safe and comfortable fold; but we are such poor good-for-nothing creatures that we have not dared to enter his fold, nor feed in this pastures. We have felt it would be presumption; and, in our humility, we have been trying to do the best we could for ourselves. The strong, healthy sheep may trust themselves to the shepherd's care, but not such miserable half-starved sheep as we are. It is true we have had a very hard time of it, and are in a sad and forlorn condition; but then we are such poor unworthy creatures that we must expect this, and must try to be resigned to it."

Silly as sheep are, we know well no sheep could be so silly as to talk in this way. And here comes the difference. We are so much wiser than sheep, in our own estimation, that we think the sort of trust sheep exercise will not do for us; and, in our superior intelligence, we presume to take matters into our own hands, and so shut ourselves out from the Shepherd's care.

Now the fact is simply this, if any sheep in the flock of Christ find themselves in a poor condition, there are only two explanations possible. Either the Lord is not a good Shepherd and does not care for His sheep, or else, His sheep have not believed in His care, and have been afraid or ashamed to trust themselves to it. I know not one of you will dare to say, or even to think, that the Lord can be anything but a good Shepherd, if He is a Shepherd at all. The fault, therefore, must lie just here; either you have not believed He was your Shepherd at all, or else, believing it, you have refused to let Him take care of you.

I entreat you to face this matter boldly, and give yourselves a definite answer. For not only your own welfare and comfort are dependent upon your right apprehension of this blessed relationship, but also the glory of your Shepherd is at stake. Have you ever thought of the grief and dishonor this sad condition of yours brings upon Him? The credit of a shepherd depends upon the condition of his flock. He might make a great boast of his qualifications as a shepherd, but it would all go for nothing if the flocks he had charge of were in a diseased condition, with many missing, and many with lean ribs and broken bones.

If an owner of sheep is thinking of employing a shepherd, he requires a reference from the shepherd's last employer, that he may learn from him how his flock fared under this shepherd's care. Now, the Lord makes statements about Himself as a good Shepherd. He is telling the universe, the world, and the Church, "I am the good shepherd"; and if they ask, "Where are Thy sheep, what condition are they in?" can He point to us as being a credit to His care? And is it not grievous if any of us refuse to let the Shepherd take care of us, and so bring discredit upon His name by our forlorn condition? The universe is looking on to see what the Lord Jesus Christ is able to make of us, and what kind of sheep we are, whether we are well fed, and healthy, and happy. Their verdict concerning Him will largely depend upon what they see in us.

When Paul was writing to the Ephesians that he had been called to preach to the Gentiles the unsearchable riches of Christ, and to make all men see what was the fellowship of the mystery which had been hid in God from the beginning of the world, he added the significant words that the object of it all was "to the intent that now unto principalities and powers in heavenly places might be known by the church the manifold wisdom of God, according to the eternal purpose which he purposed in Christ Jesus our Lord."

Well may we be lost in amazement at the thought that God has purposed such a glorious destiny for His sheep as to make known to the universe His "manifold wisdom" by means of what He has done for us! Surely this should make us eager to abandon ourselves to Him in the most generous trust for salvation to the very uttermost, that He may get great glory in the universe, and the whole world may be won to trust Him.

But if we will not let Him save us, if we reject His care, and refuse to feed in His pastures, or to lie down in His fold, then we shall be a starved and shivering flock, sick, and wretched, and full of complaints, bringing dishonor upon Him, and, by our forlorn condition, hindering the world from coming to Him.

I do not wonder that unbelievers are not drawn into the church, when I contemplate the condition of believers. I do not wonder that in some churches there are no conversions from one end of the year to the other. If I were a poor sheep, wandering in the wilderness, and I were to see some poor, wretched, sick-looking sheep peeping out of a fold, and calling me to come in, and I were to look into the fold, and should see it hard, bare, and uncomfortable, I do not think I would be much tempted to go into such a fold.

Somebody said once that some churches were too much like well-ordered graveyards: people were brought in and buried, and that was the end of it. Of course you cannot expect living people to want to take up their abodes in graveyards. We must have a fold that shows sheep in good condition if we expect outsiders to come into that fold; and if we want to attract others to the salvation of the Lord Jesus Christ, we must ourselves be able to show them that it is a satisfying and comfortable salvation. No one wants to add to their earthy discomforts by getting an uncomfortable religion, and it is useless to expect to win outsiders by the sight of our wretchedness.

Surely, if you do not care for yourselves, you cannot fail to care for the dishonor you bring upon your divine Shepherd by your poor and wretched condition. You long to serve Him, and to bring Him glory; and you can do it if you will but show to all the world that He is a Shepherd whom it is safe to trust.

Let me help you to do this. First face the fact of what a Shepherd must necessarily be and do in order to be a good Shepherd, and then face the fact that the Lord is really, and in the very highest sense of the term, a good Shepherd. Then say the words over to yourself with all the will power you can muster, "The Lord is my Shepherd. He is. He is. No matter what I feel, He says He is, and He is. I am going to believe it, come what may." Then repeat the words with a different emphasis each time:

*The Lord is my Shepherd.*
*The Lord is my Shepherd.*
*The Lord is my Shepherd.*
*The Lord is my Shepherd.*

Realize to yourself what your ideal Shepherd would be, all that you would require from anyone filling such a position of trust and of responsibility, and then know that an ideal far beyond yours, and a conception of the duties of such a position higher than any you ever dreamed of, were in the mind of our Lord when He said, "I am the good shepherd." He, better than any other, knew the sheep He had undertaken to save, and He knew the Shepherd's duties. He knew that the Shepherd is responsible for His flock, and that He is bound, at any loss of comfort, or of health, or even of life itself, to care for them and to bring them all home safely to the Master's fold. Therefore, He said: "And this is the Father's will which hath sent me that of all which he hath given me I should lose nothing, but should raise it up again at the last day." And again He said, "The good shepherd giveth his life for the sheep." And still again: "My sheep hear my voice, and I know them and they follow me, and I give unto them eternal life; and they shall never perish, neither shall any man pluck them out of my hand."

Centuries before Jesus came to be the Shepherd, the Father said: "Therefore I will save my flock. And I will set up one shepherd over them, and he shall feed them, even my servant David; he shall feed them, and he shall be their shepherd." And it seems to me, I catch a glimpse of the Father's yearning love as I read these words; and I feel sure He laid help upon One who is mighty; and that none, therefore, who are in this flock need fear any evil.

He has undertaken His duties, knowing perfectly well what the responsibilities are. He knows that He has to do with very silly sheep, who have no strength to protect themselves, no wisdom to guide themselves, and nothing to recommend them but their utter helplessness and weakness. But none of these things baffle Him. His strength and His skill are sufficient to meet every emergency that can possibly arise.

There is absolutely only one thing that can hinder Him, and that is, if the sheep will not trust Him and refuse to let Him take care of them. If they stand off at a distance, and look at the food He has provided, and long for it, and absolutely trustworthy; and nothing complicated in obedience, when we have perfect confidence in the power we are obeying.

Let me entreat you, then, to begin to trust and to follow your Shepherd now and here. Abandon yourself to His care and guidance, as a sheep in the care of a shepherd, and trust Him utterly.

You need not be afraid to follow Him whithersoever He leads, for He always leads His sheep into green pastures and beside still waters. No matter though you may seem to yourself to be in the very midst of a desert, with nothing green about you inwardly or outwardly and you may think you will have to make a long journey before you can get into any green pastures, the good Shepherd will turn the very place where you are into green pastures; for He has power to make the desert rejoice and blossom as the rose; and He has promised that "instead of the thorn shall come up the fir-tree, and instead of the briar shall come up the myrtle-tree"; and "in the wilderness shall waters break out, and streams in the desert."

Or perhaps you may say, "My life is all a tempest of sorrow or of temptation, and it will be a long while before I can walk beside any still waters." But has not your Shepherd before this said to the raging seas, "Peace! be still. And there was a great calm"? And can He not do it again?

Thousands of the flock of Christ can testify that when they have put themselves absolutely into His hands, He has quieted the raging tempest, and has turned their deserts into blossoming gardens. I do not mean that there will be no more outward trouble, or care, or suffering; but these very places will become green pastures and still waters inwardly to the soul. The Shepherd knows what pastures are best for His sheep, and they must not question or doubt, but must trustingly follow Him. Perhaps He sees that the best pastures for some of us are to be found in the midst of opposition or of earthly trials. If He leads you there, you may be sure they are green pastures for you, and that you will grow to be made strong by feeding in them.

But words fail to tell the half of what the good Shepherd does for the flock that trusts him. He does indeed, according to His promise, make with them a covenant of peace, and causes the evil beasts to cease out of the land; and they shall dwell safely in the wilderness, and sleep in the woods. And He makes them and the places round about them a blessing; and He causes the shower to come down in its season; and there are showers of blessing. And the tree of the field yields her fruit, and the earth yields her increase; and they are safe in their land, and are no more a prey to the heathen, and none can make them afraid.

And now you will probably ask me how you can get the Lord to be your Shepherd. My answer is that you do not need to get Him to be your Shepherd at all, for He already is your Shepherd. All that is needed is for you to recognize that He is, and yield yourself to His control.

When the announcement is made in a family to the children who have been longing for a little sister, that one has just been born to them, they do not go on saying, "Oh, how we wish we had a little sister!" or, "what can we do to get a little sister?" But they begin at once to shout for joy, and to dance about calling out to everybody, "Hurrah! Hurrah! We have a little sister now."

And since likewise the announcement has been made to all of us by the angel of the Lord: "Fear not, for behold I bring you good tidings of great joy, which shall be to all people. For unto you is born this day in the city of David, a Saviour which is Christ the Lord," we have no need and no right to go on crying out, "Oh, if I only had a Saviour!" or, "What shall I do to make Christ my Saviour?" He is already born our Saviour, and we must begin at once to rejoice that He is, and must give ourselves into His care. There is nothing complicated about it. It is simply to believe it, and act as if it were true. And every soul that will begin from today believing in the good Shepherd and trusting itself to His care will sooner or later find itself feeding in His green pastures, and walking beside His still waters.

What else can the Lord, who is our Shepherd, do with His sheep, but just this? He has no folds that are not good folds, no pastures that are not green pastures, and no waters but still waters. They may not look so outwardly; but we who have tried them can testify that, let the outward seeming be what it may, His fold and His pastures are always places of peace and comfort to the inward life of the soul.

If you seem to have difficulties in understanding all this, and if the life of full trust looks complicated and mysterious, I would advise you not to try to understand it, but simply to begin to live it. Just take our nursery psalm and say, "this is my psalm, and I am going to believe it. I have always known it by heart, but it has never meant much to me. But now I have made up my mind to believe that the Lord really is my Shepherd and that He will care for me as a shepherd cares for his sheep. I will not doubt nor question it again." And then just abandon yourself to His care, as the sheep abandon themselves to the care of their shepherd, trusting Him fully, and following whithersoever He leads.

But we must not forget that while sheep trust unconsciously and by instinct, we shall need to trust intelligently and of purpose for our instincts, alas, are all against trusting. We shall have to make an effort to trust. We shall have to choose to do it. But we can do this, however weak and ignorant we may be. We may not understand all it means to be a sheep of such a Shepherd, but He knows. And if our faith will but claim Him in this blessed and wondrous relationship, He will care for us according to His love, and His wisdom, and His power, and not according to our poor comprehension of it.

It really seems to me as if we did not need any other passage out of the whole Bible besides this nursery psalm to make our religious lives full of comfort. I confess I do not see where there is any room left for the believer to worry, who actually believes this psalm. With the Lord for our Shepherd, how is it possible for anything to go wrong? With Him for our Shepherd, all that this psalm promises must be ours; and when we have learned thus to know Him, we will be able to say with a triumph of trust: "Surely goodness and mercy shall follow me [pursue, overtake] all the days of my life, and I shall dwell in the house of the Lord forever." Even the future will lose all its terrors for us, and our confidence in our Shepherd will deliver us from all fear of evil tidings.

And I can only say, in conclusion, that if each one of you will just enter into this relationship with Christ, and really be a helpless, docile, trusting sheep, and will believe Him to be your Shepherd, caring for you with all the love, and care, and tenderness that that name involves, and will follow Him whithersoever He leads, you will soon lose all your old spiritual discomfort, and will know the peace of God that passeth all understanding to keep your hearts and minds in Christ Jesus.

# Chapter Five - He Spake to Them of the Father

"They understood not that he spake to them of the Father."

One of the most illuminating names of God is the one especially revealed by our Lord Jesus Christ, the name of Father. I say especially revealed by Christ, because, while God had been called throughout the ages by many other names, expressing other aspects of His character, Christ alone has revealed Him to us under the all-inclusive name of Father—a name that holds within itself all other names of wisdom and power, and above all of love and goodness, a name that embodies for us a perfect supply for all our needs. Christ, who was the only begotten Son in the bosom of the Father, was the only one who could reveal this name, for He alone knew the Father. "As the Father knoweth me," He said, "even so know I the Father" "Not that any man hath seen the Father save he which is of God, he hath seen the Father."

In the Old Testament God was not revealed as the Father so much as a great warrior fighting for His people, or as a mighty king ruling over them and caring for them. The name of Father is only given to Him a very few times there, six or seven times at the most; while in the New Testament it is given about two or three hundred times. Christ, who knew Him, was the only one who could reveal Him. "no man," He said, "knoweth who the Father is, but the Son, and he to whom the Son will reveal him."

The vital question then that confronts each one of us is whether we individually understand that Christ speaks to us of the Father. We know He uses the word Father continually, but do we in the least understand what the word means? Have we even so much as an inkling of what the Father is?

All the discomfort and unrest of the religious life of so many of God's children come, I feel sure, from this very thing, that they do not understand that God is actually and truly their Father. They think of Him as a stern Judge, or a severe Taskmaster, or at the best as an unapproachable dignitary, seated on a far-off throne, dispensing exacting laws for a frightened and trembling world; and in their terror lest they should fail to meet His requirements they hardly know which way to turn. But of a God who is a Father, tender, and loving, and full of compassion, a God who, like a father, will be on their side against the whole universe they have no conception.

I am not afraid to say that discomfort and unrest are impossible to the souls that come to know that God is their real and actual Father.

But before I go any farther I must make it plain that it is a Father, such as our highest instincts tell us a good father ought to be, of whom I am speaking. Sometimes earthly fathers are unkind, or tyrannical, or selfish, or even cruel, or they are merely indifferent and neglectful; but none of these can by any stretch of charity be called good fathers. But God, who is good, must be a good father or not a father at all. We must all of us have known good fathers in this world, or at least can imagine them. I knew one, and he filled my childhood with sunshine by his most lovely fatherhood. I can remember vividly with what confidence and triumph I walked through my days, absolutely secure in the knowledge that I had a father. And I am very sure that I have learned to know a little about the perfect fatherhood of God, because of my experience with this lovely earthly father.

But God is not only a father, He is a mother as well, and we have all of us known mothers whose love and tenderness have been without bound or limit. And it is very certain that the God who created them both, and who is Himself father and mother in one, could never have created earthly fathers and mothers who were more tender and more loving than He is Himself. Therefore if we want to know what sort of a Father He is, we must heap together all the best of all the fathers and mothers we have ever known or can imagine, and we must tell ourselves that this is only a faint image of God, our Father in Heaven.

When our Lord was teaching His disciples how to pray, the only name by which He taught them to address God was, "Our Father which art in heaven." And this surely meant that we were to think of Him only in this light. Millions upon millions of times during all the centuries since then has this name been uttered by the children of God everywhere; and yet how much has it been understood? Had all who used the name known what it meant, it would have been impossible for the misrepresentations of His character, and the doubts of His love and care, that have so desolated the souls of His children throughout all the ages, to have crept in. Tyranny, unkindness, and neglect might perhaps be attributed to a God whose name was only a king, or a judge, or a lawgiver; but of a God, who is before all else a father, and, of necessity, since He is God, a good father, no such things could possibly be believed. Moreover, since He is an "everlasting Father," He must in the very nature of things act, always and under all circumstances, as a good father ought to act, and never in any other way. It is inconceivable that a good father could forget, or neglect, or be unfair to his children. A savage father might, or a wicked father; but a good father never! And in calling our God by the blessed name of Father, we ought to know that, if He is a father at all, He must be the very best of fathers, and His fatherhood must be the highest ideal of fatherhood of which we can conceive. It is, as I have said, a fatherhood that combines both father and mother in one, in our highest ideals of both, and comprises all the love, and all the tenderness, and all the compassion, and all the yearning, and all the self-sacrifice, that we cannot but recognize to be the inmost soul of parentage, even though we may not always see it carried out by all earthly parents.

But you may say what about the other names of God, do they not convey other and more terrifying ideas? They only do so because this blessed name of Father is not added to them. This name must underlie every other name by which He has ever been known. Has He been called a Judge? Yes, but He is a Father Judge, one who judges as a loving father would. Is He a King? Yes, but He is a King who is at the same time the Father of His subjects, and who rules them with a father's tenderness. Is He a Lawgiver? Yes, but He is a Lawgiver who gives laws as a father would, remembering the weakness and ignorance of his helpless children. "Like as a father pitieth his children, so the Lord pitieth them that fear him. For he knoweth our frame; he remembereth that we are dust." It is not "as a judge judges, so the Lord judges"; not "as a taskmaster controls, so the Lord controls"; not "as a lawgiver imposes laws, so the Lord imposes laws"; but, "as a father pitieth, so the Lord pitieth."

Never, never must we think of God in any other way than as "our Father." All other attributes with which we endow Him in our conceptions must be based upon and limited by this one of "our Father." What a good father could not do, God, who is our Father, cannot do either; and what a good father ought to do, God, who is our Father, is absolutely sure to do.

In our Lord's last prayer in John 17, He says that He has declared to us the name of the Father in order that we may discover the wonderful fact that the Father loves us as He loved His Son. Now, which one of us really believes this? We have read this chapter over, I suppose, oftener than almost any other chapter in the Bible, and yet do we any of us believe that it is an actual, tangible fact, that God loves us as much as He loved Christ? If we believed this to be actually the case, could we, by any possibility, ever have an anxious or rebellious thought again? Would we not be absolutely and utterly sure always under every conceivable circumstance that the divine Father, who loves us just as much as He loved His only begotten Son, our Lord Jesus Christ, would of course care for us in the best possible way, and could not tell us so emphatically not to be anxious or troubled about anything, for He knew His Father and knew that it was safe to trust Him utterly.

It is very striking that He so often said, "Your heavenly Father, not mine only, but yours just as much. Your heavenly Father," He says, "cares for the sparrows and the lilies, and of course, therefore, he will care for you who are of so much more value than many sparrows." How supremely foolish it is then for us to be worried and anxious about things, when Christ has said that our heavenly Father knows that we have need of all these things! For of course, being a good father, He must in the very nature of the case, when He knows our need, supply it.

What can be the matter with us that we do not understand this?

Again, our Lord draws the comparison between earthly fathers and our heavenly Father, in order to show us, not how much less good and tender and willing to bless is our heavenly Father, but how much more. "if ye, being evil," He says, "know how to give good gifts unto your children, how much more shall your Father which is in heaven give good things to them that ask him." Can we conceive of a good earthly father giving a stone or a serpent to a hungry child instead of bread or fish? Would not our whole souls revolt from a father who could do such things? And yet, I fear, there are a great many of God's children who actually think that their heavenly Father does this sort of thing to them, and gives them stones when they ask for bread, or curses when they ask for blessings. And perhaps these very people may belong to the Society for the Prevention of Cruelty to Children, a society which is the nation's protest against such behavior on the part of earthly fathers; and yet they never have thought of the dreadful wickedness of charging their heavenly Father with things which they are banded together to punish in earthly fathers!

But it is not only that our heavenly Father is willing to give us good things. He is far more than willing. Our Lord says, "Fear not, little flock, it is your Father's good pleasure to give you the kingdom." There is no grudging in His giving, it is His "good pleasure" to give; He likes to do it. He wants to give you the kingdom far more than you want to have it. Those of us who are parents know how eager we are to give good things to our children, often far more eager than our children are to have them; and this may help us to understand how it is that it is God's "good pleasure" to give us the kingdom. Why, then, should we ask Him in such fear and trembling, and why should we torment ourselves with anxiety lest He should fail to grant what we need?

There can be only one answer to these questions, and that is, that we do not know the Father.

We are told that we are of the "household of God." Now the principle is announced in the Bible that if any man provides not for his own household, he has "denied the faith and is worse than an infidel." Since then we are of the "household of God," this principle applies to Him, and if He should fail to provide for us, His own words would condemn Him. I say this reverently, but I want to say it emphatically, for so few people seem to have realized it.

It was in my own case a distinct era of immense importance when I first discovered this fact of the responsibility of my Father in Heaven. As it were, in a single moment, the burden of life was lifted off my shoulders and laid on His, and all my fears, and anxieties, and questionings dropped into the abyss of His loving care. I saw that the instinct of humanity, which demands that the parents who bring a child into the world are bound by every law, both human and divine, to care for and protect that child according to their best ability, is a divinely implanted instinct; and that it is meant to teach us the magnificent fact that the

Creator, who has made human parents responsible toward their children, is Himself equally responsible toward His children. I could have shouted for joy! And from that glad hour my troubles were over. For when this insight comes to a soul, that soul must, in the very nature of things, enter into rest.

With such a God, who is at the same time a Father, there is no room for anything but rest. And when, ever since that glad day, temptations to doubt or anxiety or fear have come to me, I have not dared in the fact of what I then learned to listen to them, because I have seen that to do so would be to cast a doubt on the trustworthiness of my Father in Heaven.

We may have been accustomed to think that our doubts and fears were because of our own unworthiness and arose from humility; and we may even have taken them as a sign of especial piety, and have thought they were in some way pleasing to God. But if, in their relations with their earthly parents, children should let in doubts of their love, and fears lest their care should fail, would these doubts and fears be evidences of filial piety on the children's part, and would they be at all pleasing to their parents?

If God is our Father, the only thing we can do with doubts, and fears, and anxious thoughts is to cast them behind our backs forever, and have nothing more to do with them ever again. We can do this. We can give up our doubts just as we would urge a drunkard to give up his drink. We can pledge against doubting. And if once we see that our doubts are an actual sin against God, and imply a question of His trustworthiness, we will be eager to do it. We may have cherished our doubts heretofore because perhaps we have thought they were a part of our religion, and a becoming attitude of soul in one so unworthy; but if we now see that God is in very truth our Father, we will reject every doubt with horror, as being a libel on our Father's love and our Father's care.

What more can any soul want than to have a God whose name is "our Father," and whose character and ways must name? As Philip said, so we find it to be, "Show us the Father and it sufficeth us." It does indeed suffice, beyond what words can express!

A friend of mine went one day to see a poor negro woman living in one of the poorest parts of Philadelphia, whose case had been reported to her as being one of great need. She found things even worse than she had feared. The poor woman was old, crippled with rheumatism, and lived alone in a poor little room with only the help of a kind neighbor now and then to do things for her; and yet she was bright and cheerful, and full of thanksgiving for her many mercies. My friend marveled that cheerfulness or thankfulness could be possible under such circumstances, and said, "But do you never get frightened at the thought of what may happen to you, all alone here, and so lame as you are?"

The old negro saint looked at her with surprise, and said in a tone of the utmost amazement, "Frightened! Why, honey, doesn't you know I have got a Father, and doesn't you know He takes care of me the whole endurin' time?" And then, as my friend looked perplexed, she added in a tone of wondering reproof, "Why, honey, sholy my Father is your Father too, and you knows about Him, and you knows He always takes care of His chilluns." It was a lesson my friend never forgot.

"Behold," says the apostle John, "what manner of love the Father hath bestowed upon us, that we should be called the sons of God." The "manner of love" bestowed upon us is the love of a father for his son, a tender protecting love, that knows our weakness and our need, and cares for us accordingly. He treats us as sons, and all He asks in return is that we shall treat Him as a Father, whom we can trust without anxiety. We must take the son's place of dependence and trust, and must let Him keep the father's place of care and responsibility. Because we are the children and He is the Father, we must let Him do the father's part. Too often we take upon our own shoulders the father's part, and try to take care of and provide for ourselves. But no good earthy father would want his children to take upon their young shoulders the burden of his duties, and surely much less would our heavenly Father want to lay upon us the burden of His.

No wonder we are told to cast all our care upon Him, for He careth for us. He careth for us; of course He does. It is His business, as a Father, to do so. He would not be a good Father if He did not. All He asks of us is to let Him know when we need anything, and then leave the supplying of that need to Him; and He assures us that if we do this the "peace of God that passeth all understanding shall keep our hearts and minds." The children of a good, human father are at peace because they trust in their father's care; but the children of the heavenly Father too often have no peace because they are afraid to trust in His care. They make their requests known to Him perhaps, but that is all they do. It is a sort of religious form they feel it necessary to go through. But as to supposing that He really will care for them, no such idea seems to cross their minds; and they go on carrying their cares and burdens on their own shoulders, exactly as if they had no Father in Heaven, and had never asked him to care for them.

What utter folly it all is! For if ever an earthly father was worthy of the confidence of his children, surely much more is our heavenly Father worthy of our confidence. And why it is that so few of His children trust Him can only be because they have not yet found out that He is really their Father; or else that, calling Him Father every day in their prayers, they still have never seen that He is the sort of Father a good and true human father is, a Father who is loving, and tender, pitiful, and full of kindness toward the helpless beings whom He has brought into existence, and whom He is therefore bound to protect. This sort of Father no one could help trusting; but the strange and far-off Creator, whose fatherhood stops at our creation, and has no care for our fate after once we are launched into the universe, no one could be expected to trust.

The remedy, therefore, for your discomfort and unrest is to be found in becoming acquainted with the Father.

"For," says the apostle, "ye have not received the spirit of bondage again to fear; but ye have received the spirit of adoption, whereby we cry, Abba, Father." Is it this "spirit of adoption" that reigns in your hearts, my readers, or is it the "spirit of bondage"? Your whole comfort in the religious life depends upon which spirit it is; and no amount of wrestling or agonizing, no prayers, and no efforts will be able to bring you comfort, while the "spirit of adoption" is lacking in your heart.

But you may ask how you are to get this "spirit of adoption." I can only say that it is not a thing to be gotten. It comes; and it comes as the necessary result of the discovery that God is in very truth a real Father. When we have made this discovery, we cannot help feeling and acting like a child; and this is what the "spirit of adoption" means. It is nothing mystical nor mysterious; it is the simple natural result of having found a Father where you thought there was only a Judge.

The great need for every soul, therefore, is to make this supreme discovery. And to do this we have only to see what Christ tells us about the Father, and then believe it. "Verily, verily," He declares, "I say unto thee, We speak that we do know, and testify that we have seen," but, He adds sadly, "ye receive not our witness." In order to come to the knowledge of the Father, we must receive the testimony of Christ, who declares: "The words that I speak unto you I speak not of myself; but the Father that dwelleth in me, he doeth the works." Over and over He repeated this, and in John, after grieving over the fact that so few received his testimony, He adds these memorable words: "He that hath received his testimony hath set to his seal that God is true."

The whole authority of Christ stands or falls with this. If we receive His testimony, we set to our seal that God is true. If we reject that testimony, we make Him a liar.

"If ye had known me," says Christ, "ye should have known my Father also; and from henceforth ye know him, and have seen him." The thing for us to do then is to make up our minds that from henceforth we will receive His testimony, and will "know the Father." Let other people worship whatever sort of a God they may, for us there must be henceforth "but one God, even the Father."

"For though there be that are called gods, whether in heaven or in earth (as there be gods many, and lords many), but to us there is but one God, the Father, of whom are all things, and we in him; and one Lord Jesus Christ, by whom are all things, and we by him."

# Chapter Six - Jehovah

"That men may know that thou, whose name alone is Jehovah, art the most High over all the earth."

Among all the names of God perhaps the most comprehensive is the name Jehovah. Cruden describes this name as the incommunicable name of God. The word Jehovah means the self-existing One, the "I am"; and it is generally used as a direct revelation of what God is. In several places an explanatory word is added, revealing some one of His special characteristics; and it is to these that I want particularly to call attention. They are as follows:

Jehovah-jireh, i.e., The Lord will see, or the Lord will provide.

Jehovah-nissi, i.e., The Lord my Banner.

Jehovah-shalom, i.e., The Lord our Peace.

Jehovah-tsidkenu, i.e., The Lord our Righteousness.

Jehovah-shammah, i.e., The Lord is there.

These names were discovered by God's people in times of sore need; that is, the characteristics they describe were discovered, and the names were the natural expression of these characteristics.

When Abraham was about to sacrifice his son, and saw no way of escape, the Lord provided a lamb for the sacrifice and delivered Isaac; and Abraham made the grand discovery that it was one of the characteristics of Jehovah to see and provide for the needs of His people. Therefore he called Him Jehovah-jireh—the Lord will see, or the Lord will provide.

The counterparts to this in the New Testament are very numerous. Over and over our Lord urges us to take no care, because God careth for us. "Your heavenly Father knoweth," He says, "that ye have need of all these things." If the Lord sees and knows our need, it will be a matter of course with Him to provide for it. Being our Father, He could not do anything else. As soon as a good mother sees that her child needs anything, at once she sets about supplying that need. She does not even wait for the child to ask, the sight of the need is asking enough. Being a good mother, she could not do otherwise.

When God, therefore, says to us, "I am he that seeth thy need," He in reality says also, "I am he that provideth," for He cannot see, and fail to provide.

"Why do I not have everything I want, then?" you may ask. Only because God sees that what you want is not really the thing you need, but probably exactly the opposite. Often, in order to give us what we need, the Lord is obliged to keep from us what we want. Your heavenly Father knoweth what things ye have need of, you do not know; and were all your wants gratified, it might well be that all your needs would be left unsupplied. It surely ought to suffice us that our God is indeed Jehovah-jireh, the Lord who will see, and who will therefore provide.

But I am afraid a great many Christians of the present day have never made Abraham's discovery, and do not know that the Lord is really Jehovah-jirah. They are trusting Him, it may be, to save their souls in the future, but they never dream He wants to carry their cares for them now and here. They are like a man I have heard of, with a heavy load on his back, who was given a lift by a friend, and who thankfully availed himself of it. Climbing into the conveyance, but still keeping his burden on his back, he sat there bowed down under the weight of it. "Why do you not put your burden down on the bottom of the carriage?" asked his friend.

"Oh," replied the man, "it is a great deal to ask you to carry me myself, and I could not ask you to carry my burden also." You wonder that anyone could be so foolish, and yet are you not doing the same? Are you not trusting the Lord to take care of yourself, but are still going on carrying your burdens on your own shoulders? Which is the silliest—that man or you?

Jehovah-nissi, i.e., "The Lord my banner," was a discovery made by Moses when Amalek came to fight with Israel in Rephidim, and the Lord gave the Israelites a glorious victory. Moses realized that the Lord was fighting for them, and he built an altar to Jehovah-nissi, "The Lord my banner." The Bible is full of developments of this name. "The Lord is a man of war"; "The Lord your God, he it is that fighteth for you"; "The Lord shall fight for you, and ye shall hold your peace"; "Be not afraid nor dismayed, by reason of this great multitude, for the battle is not yours, but God's"; "God himself is with us for our captain."

Nothing is more abundantly proved in the Bible than this, that the Lord will fight for us if we will but let Him. He knows that we have no strength nor might against our spiritual enemies; and, like a tender mother when her helpless children are attacked by an enemy, He fights for us; and all He asks of us is to be still and let Him. This is the only sort of spiritual conflict that is ever successful. But we are very slow to learn this, and when temptations come, instead of handing the battle over to the Lord, we summon all our forces to fight them ourselves. We believe, perhaps, that the Lord is somewhere near, and, if the worst comes to the worst, will step in to help us; but for the most part we feel that we ourselves, and we only, must do all the fighting. Our method of fighting consists generally in a series of repentings, and making resolutions and promises, and weary struggles for victory, and then failing again; and again repentance, and resolutions, and promises, and renewed struggles, and all this over, and over, and over again, each time telling ourselves that now at last we certainly will have the victory, and each time failing even worse than before. And this may go on for weeks, or months, or even years, and no real or permanent deliverance ever comes.

But you may ask, "Are we not to do any fighting ourselves?" Of course we are to fight, but not in this fashion. We are to fight the "good fight of faith," as Paul exhorted Timothy; and the fight of faith is not a fight of effort or of struggle, but it is a fight of trusting. It is the kind of fight that Hezekiah fought when he and his army marched out to meet their enemy, singing songs of victory as they went, and finding their enemy all dead men. Our part in this fight is to hand the battle over to the Lord, and to trust Him for the victory.

And we are to put on His armor, not our own. The apostle tells us what it is. It is the girdle of truth, and the breastplate of righteousness, and the preparation of the gospel of peace on our feet, and the helmet of salvation, and the sword of the Spirit which is the Word of God; but above all, he says, we are to take the shield of faith wherewith we shall be able to quench all the fiery darts of the wicked.

There is nothing here about promises or resolutions; nothing about hours and days of agonizing struggles, and of bitter remorse. "Above all things taking the shield of faith." Above all things faith. Faith is the one essential thing, without which all else is useless. And it means that we must not only hand the battle over to the Lord, but we must leave it with Him, and must have absolute faith that He will conquer. It is here where the fight comes in. It seems so unsafe to sit still, and do nothing but trust the Lord; and the temptation to take the battle back into our own hands is often tremendous. To keep hands off in spiritual matters is as hard for us as it is for the drowning man to keep hands off the one who is trying to rescue him. We all know how impossible it is to rescue a drowning man who tries to help his rescuer, and it is equally impossible for the Lord to fight our battles for us when we insist upon trying to fight them ourselves. It is not that He will not, but He cannot. Our interference hinders His working. Spiritual forces cannot work while earthly forces are active.

Our Lord tells us that without Him we can do nothing, and we have read and repeated His words hundreds of times; but does anyone really believe they are actually true? If we should drag out into the light our secret thoughts on the subject, should we not find them to be something like this: "When Christ said those words He meant of course to say that we cannot of ourselves do much, or at any rate no great things. But nothing; ah, no, that is impossible. We are not babies, and we are certainly meant to use all the strength we have in fighting our enemies; and, when our own strength gives out, we can then call upon the Lord to help us." In spite of all our failures, we cannot help thinking that, if only we should try harder and be more persistent, we should be equal to any encounter. But we entirely overlook the vital fact that our natural powers are of no avail in spiritual regions or with spiritual enemies. The grub of the dragonfly, that lives at the bottom of the pond, may be a finely developed and vigorous grub; but, when it becomes a dragonfly, the powers of its grub life, that availed for creeping about in the mud, would be useless for winging its flight in the free air.

And just as our skill in walking on the earth would avail us nothing if we had to fly in the air, so our natural powers are of no avail in spiritual warfare. They are, in fact, if we try to depend on them, real hindrances, just as trying to walk would hinder us, if we sought to float or to fly. We can easily see, therefore, that the result of trusting in ourselves, when dealing with our spiritual enemies, must inevitable be very serious. It not only causes failure, but in the end it causes rebellion; and a great deal of what is called "spiritual conflict" might far better be named "spiritual rebellion." God has told us to cease from our own efforts, and to hand our battles over to Him, and we point blank refuse to obey Him. We fight, it is true, but it is not a fight of faith, but a fight of unbelief. Our spiritual "wrestling," of which we are often so proud, is really a wrestling, not for God against His enemies, but against Him on the side of His enemies. We allow ourselves to indulge in doubts and fears, and as a consequence we are plunged into darkness, and turmoil, and wrestlings of spirit. And then we call this "spiritual conflict," and look upon ourselves as an interesting and "peculiar case." The single word that explains our "peculiar case" is the word unbelief, and the simple remedy is to be found in the word faith.

But you may ask, what about "wrestling Jacob"? Did he not gain his victory by wrestling? To this I reply, that on the contrary he gained his victory by being made so weak that he could not wrestle any longer. It was not Jacob who wrestled with the angel, but the angel who wrestled with Jacob. Jacob was the one to be overcome; and when the angel found that Jacob's resistance was so great that he could not "prevail against him," he was obliged to make him lame by putting his thigh out of joint; and then the victory was won. As soon as Jacob was too weak to resist any longer, he prevailed with God. He gained power when he lost it. He conquered when he could no longer fight.

Jacob's experience is ours. The Lord wrestles with us in order to bring us to a place of entire dependence on Him. We resist as long as we have any strength; until at last He is forced to bring us to a place of helplessness, where we are obliged to yield; and then we conquer by this very yielding. Our victory is always the victory of weakness. Paul knew this victory when he said: "And the Lord said unto me, My grace is sufficient for thee; for my strength is made perfect in weakness. Most gladly therefore will I rather glory in my infirmities, that the power of Christ may rest upon me. Therefore I take pleasure in infirmities, in reproaches, in necessities, in persecutions, in distresses for Christ's sake; for when I am weak, then am I strong."

Who would ask for a more magnificent victory than this!

And this victory will be ours, if we take the Lord to be our Banner, and commit all our battles to Him.

The name of Jehovah-shalom, or "The Lord our peace," was discovered by Gideon when the Lord had called him to a work for which he felt himself to be utterly unfitted. "Oh, my Lord," he had said, "wherewith shall I save Israel? Behold, my family is poor in Manasseh, and I am the least of my father's house." And the Lord answered him, saying: "Surely I will be with thee, and thou shalt smite the Midianites as one man ... And the Lord said unto him, Peace be unto thee: fear not; for thou shalt not die." Then Gideon believed the Lord; and, although the battle had not yet been fought, and no victories had been won, with the eye of faith he saw peace already secured and he built an altar unto the Lord, and called it Jehovah-shalom, i.e., "The Lord our peace."

Of all the needs of the human heart none is greater than the need for peace; and none is more abundantly promised in the Gospel. "Peace I leave with you," says our Lord, "my peace I give unto you. Let not your heart be troubled, neither let it be afraid." And again He says: "These things have I spoken unto you, that in me ye might have peace. In the world ye shall have tribulation: but be of good cheer, I have overcome the world."

Our idea of peace is that it must be outward before it can be inward, that all enemies must be driven away, and all troubles cease. But the Lord's idea was of an interior peace that could exist in the midst of turmoil, and could be triumphant over it. And the ground of this sort of peace is found in the fact, not that we have overcome the world, or that we ever can, but that Christ has overcome it. Only the conqueror can proclaim peace, and the people, whose battles He has fought, can do nothing but enter into it. They can neither make nor unmake it. But, if they choose, they can refuse to believe in it, and so can fail to let it reign in their hearts. You may be afraid to believe that Christ has made peace for you, and so may live on in a weary state of warfare; but nevertheless, He has done it, and all your continued warfare is worse than useless.

The Bible tells us that Christ is our peace, and consequently, whether I feel as if I had peace or not, peace is really mine in Christ, and I must take possession of it by faith. Faith is simply to believe and assert the thing that God says. If He says there is peace, faith asserts that there is, and enters into the enjoyment of it. If He has proclaimed peace in the Bible, I must proclaim it in my own heart, let the seemings be what they may. "The kingdom of God is righteousness, peace, and joy, in the Holy Ghost," and the soul that has not taken possession of peace has not yet fully entered into this kingdom.

Practically I believe we can always enter into peace by a simple obedience to Philippians 4:6,7: "Be careful for nothing; but in everything by prayer and supplication with thanksgiving let your requests be made known unto God. And the peace of God, which passeth all understanding, shall keep your hearts and minds through Christ Jesus." The steps here are very plain, and they are only two. First, give up all anxiety; and second, hand over your cares to God; and then stand steadfastly here; peace must come. It simply must, for there is no room for anything else.

The name Jehovah-tsidkenu, "The Lord our righteousness," was revealed by the Lord Himself through the mouth of the prophet Jeremiah, when he was announcing the coming of Christ. "Behold, the day is come, saith the Lord, that I will raise unto David a righteous Branch, and a King shall reign and prosper, and shall execute judgment and justice in the earth. In his days Judah shall be saved, and Israel shall dwell safely, and this is the name whereby he shall be called, Jehovah-tsidkenu, The Lord our righteousness."

Greater than any other need is our need for righteousness. Most of the struggles and conflicts of our Christian life come from our fights with sin, and our efforts after righteousness. And I need not say how great are our failures. As long as we try to conquer sin or attain to righteousness by our own efforts, we are bound to fail. But if we discover that the Lord is our righteousness, we shall have the secret of victory. In the Lord Jesus Christ we have a fuller revelation of this wonderful name of God. The apostle Paul in his character as the "ambassador for Christ" declares that God hath made Christ to be sin for us, that we might be made the righteousness of God in Him. And again he says that Christ is made unto us wisdom, and righteousness, and sanctification, and redemption. I am afraid that very few Christians really understand what this means. We repeat the words as belonging to our religious vocabulary, and in a vague sort of way think of them as being somehow a part of the salvation of Christ, but what part or of what practical use we have very little real idea.

To me this name of God, the Lord our righteousness, seems of such tremendously practical use that I want if possible to make it plain to others. But it is difficult; and I cannot possibly explain it theologically. But experimentally it seems to me like this: We are not to try to have a stock of righteousness laid up in ourselves, from which to draw a supply when needed, but we are to draw continual fresh supplies as we need them from the righteousness that is laid up for us in Christ. I mean, that if we need righteousness of any sort, such as patience, or humility, or love, it is useless for us to look within, hoping to find a supply there, for we never will find it; but we must simply take it by faith, as a possession that is stored up for us in Christ, who is our righteousness. If I cannot tell theologically how this is done, I know experimentally that it can be done, and that the results are triumphant. I have seen sweetness and gentleness poured like a flood of sunshine into dark and bitter spirits, when the hand of faith has been reached out to grasp them as a present possession, stored up for all who need in Christ. I have seen sharp tongues made tender, anxious hearts made calm, and fretful spirits made quiet by the simple step of taking by faith the righteousness that is ours in Christ.

The apostle, after proving to us in the third chapter of Romans the absolute impossibility of any satisfying righteousness coming to us by the law (that is, by our own efforts) goes on to say: "But now the righteousness of God without the law is manifested, being witnessed by the law and the prophets, even the righteousness of God which is by faith of Jesus Christ unto all and upon all them that believe; for there is no difference."

It is faith and faith only that can appropriate this righteousness that is ours in Christ. Just as we appropriate by faith the forgiveness that is ours in Christ, so must we appropriate by faith the patience that is ours in Him, or the gentleness, or the meekness, or the long-suffering, or any other virtue we may need. Our own efforts will not procure righteousness for us, any more than they will procure forgiveness. And yet how many Christians try! Paul describes them when he says: "For I bear them record that they have a zeal of God, but not according to knowledge. For they being ignorant of God's righteousness, and going about to establish their own righteousness, have not submitted themselves unto the righteousness of God. For Christ is the end of the law for righteousness to every one that believeth."

Would that all such zealous souls could discover this wonderful name of God, "The Lord our righteousness," and would give up at once and forever seeking to establish their own righteousness, and would submit themselves to the righteousness of God. The prophet tells us that our own righteousness, even if we could attain to any, is nothing but filthy rags; and Paul prays that he may be found in Christ, not having his own righteousness, which is of the law, but that which is through the faith of Christ, the righteousness which is of God by faith.

Do we at all comprehend the meaning of this prayer? And are we prepared to join in it with our whole hearts? If so, our struggle after righteousness will be over. Jehovah-tsidkenu will supply all our needs.

The name Jehovah-shammah, or "the Lord is there," was revealed to the prophet Ezekiel when he was shown by a vision, the twenty-fifth year of their captivity, what was to be the future home of the children of Israel. He described the land and the city of Jerusalem, and ended his description by saying: "And the name of that city shall be called Jehovah-shammah, or the Lord is there."

To me this name includes all the others. Wherever the Lord is, all must go right for His children. Where the good mother is, all goes right, up to the measure of her ability, for her children. And how much more God. His presence is enough. We can all remember how the simple presence is enough. We can all remember how the simple presence of our mothers was enough for us when we were children. All that we needed of comfort, rest, and deliverance was insured to us by the mere fact of our mother, as she sat in her accustomed chair with her work, or her book, or her writing, and we had burst in upon her with our doleful budget of childish woes. If we could but see that the presence of God is the same assurance of comfort, and rest, and deliverance, only infinitely more so, a well-spring of joy would be opened up in our religious lives that would drive out every vestige of discomfort and distress.

All through the Old Testament the Lord's one universal answer to all the fears and anxieties of the children of Israel was the simple words, "I will be with thee." He did not need to say anything more. His presence was to them a perfect guarantee that all their needs would be supplied; and the moment they were assured of it, they were no longer afraid to face the fiercest foe.

You may say, "Ah, yes, if the Lord would only say the same thing to me, I should not be afraid either." Well, He has said it, and has said it in unmistakable terms. When the "angel of the Lord" announced to Joseph the coming birth of Christ, he said: "They shall call his name Emmanuel; which being interpreted is, God with us." In this short sentence is revealed to us the grandest fact the world can ever know—that God, the Almighty God, the Creator of Heaven and earth, is not a far-off God, dwelling in a Heaven of unapproachable glory, but has come down in Christ to dwell with us right here in this world, in the midst of our poor, ignorant, helpless lives, as close to us as we are to ourselves. If we believe in Christ at all, we are shut up to believing this, for this is His name, "God with us."

Both these names then, Jehovah-shammah and Emmanuel, mean the same thing. They mean that God is everywhere present in His universe, surrounding everything, and sustaining everything, and holding all of us in His safe and blessed keeping. They mean that we can find no place in all His universe of which it cannot be said, "The Lord is there." The psalmist says: "Whither shall I go from thy spirit? And whither shall I flee from thy presence? If I ascend up into heaven, thou art there; if I make my bed in hell, behold, thou art there. If I take the wings of the morning, and dwell in the uttermost parts of the sea, even there shall thy hand lead me, and thy right hand shall hold me."

We cannot drift from the love and care of an ever-present God. And those Christians who think He has forsaken them, and who cry out for His presence, are crying out in ignorance of the fact that He is always and everywhere present with them. In truth they cannot get out of His presence, even should they try. Oh, that they knew this wonderful and satisfying name of God!

Speak to Him, thou, for He hears; and spirit with spirit may meet; Closer is He than breathing, and nearer than hands and feet.

Let us sum up, once more, the teaching of these five names of God. What is it they say to us?

Jehovah-jireh, i.e., "I am he who sees thy need, and therefore provides for it."

Jehovah-nissi, i.e., "I am the captain, and thy banner, and he who will fight thy battles for thee."

Jehovah-shalom, i.e., "I am thy peace. I have made peace for thee, and my peace I give unto thee."

Jehovah-tsidkenu, i.e., "I am thy righteousness. In me thou wilt find all thou needest of wisdom, and righteousness, and sanctification, and redemption."

Jehovah-shammah, i.e., "I am with thee. I am thy ever-present, all-environing God and Saviour. I will never leave thee nor forsake thee. Wherever thou goest, there I am, and there shall my hand hold thee, and my right hand lead thee."

All this is true, whether we know it and recognize it or not. We may never have dreamed that God was such a God as this, and we may have gone through our lives thus far starved, and weary, and wretched. But all the time we have been starving in the midst of plenty. The fullness of God's salvation has awaited our faith; and "abundance of grace and of the gift of righteousness" have awaited our receiving.

Would that I could believe that for some of my readers all this was ended, and that henceforth they would see that these all-embracing names of God leave no tiny corner of their need unsupplied. Then would they be able to testify with the prophet to all around them: "Behold, God is my salvation: for the Lord Jehovah is my strength and my song; he also is become my salvation. Therefore with joy shall we draw water out of the wells of salvation."

# Chapter Seven - "The Lord Is Good"

"O taste and see that the Lord is good; blessed is the man that trusteth in him."

Have you ever asked yourself what you honestly think of God down at the bottom of your heart whether you believe Him to be a good God or a bad God? I dare say the question will shock you, and you will be horrified at the suggestion that you could by any possibility think that God is a bad God. But before you have finished this chapter, I suspect some of you will be forced to acknowledge that, unconsciously perhaps, but nonetheless truly, you have, by your doubts and your upbraiding, attributed to Him a character that you would be horrified to have attributed to yourself.

I shall never forget the hour when I first discovered that God was really good. I had, of course, always known that the Bible said He was good, but I had thought it only meant He was religiously good; and it had never dawned on me that it meant He was actually and practically good, with the same kind of goodness He has commanded us to have. The expression, "The goodness of God," had seemed to me nothing more than a sort of heavenly statement, which I could not be expected to understand. And then one day I came in my reading of the Bible across the words, "O taste and see that the Lord is good," and suddenly they meant something. The Lord is good, I repeated to myself. What does it mean to be good? What but this, the living up to the best and highest that one knows. To be good is exactly the opposite of being bad. To be bad is to know the right and not to do it, but to be good is to do the best we know. And I saw that, since God is omniscient, He must know what is the best and highest good of all, and that therefore His goodness must necessarily be beyond question. I can never express what this meant to me. I had such a view of the real actual goodness of God that I saw nothing could possibly go wrong under His care, and it seemed to me that no one could ever be anxious again. And over and over, when appearance have been against Him, and when I have been tempted to question whether He had not been unkind, or neglectful, or indifferent, I have been brought up short by the words, "The Lord is good"; and I have seen that it was simply unthinkable that a God who was good could have done the bad things I had imagined.

You shrink with horror, perhaps, from the suggestion that you could under any circumstances, even in the secret depths of your heart, attribute to God what was bad. And yet you do not hesitate to accuse Him of doing things, which if one of your friends should do them, you would look upon as most dishonorable and unkind. For instance, Christians get into trouble; all looks dark, and they have no sense of the Lord's presence. They begin to question whether the Lord has not forsaken them, and sometimes even accuse Him of indifference and neglect. And they never realize that these accusations are tantamount to saying that the Lord does not keep His promises, and does not treat them as kindly and honorable as they expect all their human friends to treat them. If one of our human friends should forsake us because we were in trouble, we would consider such a friend as very far from being good. How is it, then, that we can even for one moment accuse our Lord of such actions? No, dear friend, if the Lord is good, not pious only, but really good, it must be because He always under every circumstance acts up to the highest ideal of that which He Himself has taught us is goodness. Goodness in Him must mean, just as it does with us, the living up to the best and highest He knows.

Practically, then, it means that He will not neglect any of His duties toward us, and that He will always treat us in the best possible way. This may sound like a platitude, and you may exclaim, "Why tell us this, for it is what we all believe?" But do you? If you did, would it be possible for you ever to think He was neglectful, or indifferent, or unkind, or self-absorbed, or inconsiderate? Do not put on a righteous air, and say, "Oh, but I never do accuse Him of any such things. I would not dare to." Do you not? Have you never laid to His charge things you would scorn to do yourselves? How was it when that last grievous disappointment came? Did you not feel as if the Lord had been unkind in permitting such a thing to come upon you, when you were trying so hard to serve Him? Do you never look upon His will as a tyrannical and arbitrary will, that must be submitted to, or course, but that could not by any possibility be loved? Does it never seem to you a hard thing to say, "Thy will be done"? But could it seem hard if you really believed that the Lord is good, and that He always does that which is good?

The Lord Jesus took great care to tell us that He was a good Shepherd, because He knew how often appearances would be against Him, and how tempted we should be to question His goodness. "I am a good Shepherd," He says in effect, "not a bad one. Bad shepherds neglect and forsake their sheep, but I am a good Shepherd, and never neglect nor forsake My sheep. I give My life for the sheep." His ideal of goodness in a shepherd was that the shepherd must protect the sheep entrusted to his care, even at the cost of his own life; and He came up to His own ideal. Now, can we not see that if we really believe that He is good, not in some mysterious, religious way, but in this common-sense, human way, we shall be brought out into a large place of peace and comfort at once. If I am a sheep, and the Lord is a good Shepherd, in the ordinary common-sense definition of good, how utterly secure I am! How sure I may be of the best of care in every respect! How safe I am for time and for eternity!

Let us be honest with ourselves. Have we never in our secret hearts accused the Lord of the characteristics that He has told us in Ezekiel are the marks of a bad shepherd. Have we not thought that He cared for His own comfort or glory more than He cared for ours? Have we not complained that He has not strengthened us when we were weak, or bound up our broken hearts, or sought for us when we were lost? Have we not even actually looked upon our diseased, and helpless, and lost condition, as a reason why He would not any longer have anything to do with us? In what does this differ from if we should say out plump and plain, the Lord is a bad shepherd, and does not fulfill His duties to His sheep. You shrink in horror, perhaps, at this translation of your inward murmurings and complainings, but what else, I ask you, can they in all honesty mean? It is of vital importance now and then to drag out our secret thoughts and feelings about the Lord into the full light of the Holy Spirit, that we may see what our attitude about Him really is. It is fatally easy to get into a habit of wrong thoughts about God, thoughts which will insensibly separate us from Him by a wide gulf of doubt and unbelief. More than anything else, more even than sin, wrong thoughts about God sap the foundations of our spiritual life, and grieve His heart of love. We can understand this from ourselves. Nothing grieves us so much as to have our friends misjudge and misunderstand us, and attribute to us motives we scorn. And nothing, I believe, so grieves the Lord. It is, in fact, idolatry. For what is idolatry but creating and worshipping a false God, and what are we doing but this very thing, when we allow ourselves to misjudge Him, and attribute to Him actions and feelings that are unkind and untrustworthy.

It is called in the Bible a speaking against God. "Yea, they spake against God; they said, Can God furnish a table in the wilderness?" This seemed a very innocent question to ask. But God had promised to supply all their needs in the wilderness; and to ask this question implied a secret want of confidence in His ability to do as He had promised; and it was therefore, in spite of its innocent appearance, a real "speaking against" Him. A good God could not have led His people into the wilderness, and then have failed to "furnish a table" for them; and to question whether He was able to do it was to imply that He was not good. In the same way we are sometimes sorely tempted to ask a similar question. Circumstances often seem to make it so impossible for God to supply our needs, that we find ourselves tempted over and over to "speak against" Him by asking if He can. Often as He has done it before, we seem unable to believe He can do it again, and in our hearts we "limit" Him, because we do not believe His Word or trust in His goodness.

If our faith were what it ought to be, no circumstances, however untoward, could make us "limit" the power of God to supply our needs. The God who can make circumstances can surely control circumstances, and can, even in the wilderness, "furnish a table" for all who trust in Him.

There are many similar questions to be found in the Bible, each one throwing doubts upon the goodness of God, and each one, I am afraid, is a duplicate of questions asked by God's children now.

"Is God among us or not?"

"Hath God forgotten to be gracious?"

"Is God's mercy clean gone forever?"

"Hath God in anger shut up his tender mercies?"

"Do God's promises fail forevermore?"

"O God, why hast thou cast us off forever?"

"Why hast thou made me thus?"

Let us consider these questions for a little, and see whether we can find any counterparts to them in our own secret questionings.

"Is God among us or not?"

He has declared to us in unmistakable terms, as He did to the children of Israel, that He is always with us, and will never forsake us; and yet when trouble comes, we begin, as they did, to doubt His Word and to question whether He really can be there. Moses called this, when the Israelites did it, "tempting the Lord," and it deserves the same condemnation when we do it. No one can ask such a question without casting a doubt upon the truthfulness and trustworthiness of the Lord; and to ask it is, if we only knew it, to insult Him, and to libel His character. I know that it is, alas! a common question even among God's own children, and I know also that many of them think it is only true humility to ask it, and that, for such unworthy creatures as they feel themselves to be, it would be the height of presumption to be sure of His presence with them. But what about His own Word in the matter? He has declared to us in every possible way that He is with us, and will never leave us nor forsake us, and dare we "make him a liar" by questioning the truth of His Word? A good God cannot lie, and we must give up forever asking such a question as this. The Lord is with us as truly as we are with ourselves, and we have simply just got to believe that He is, no matter what the seemings may be.

"Hath God forgotten to be gracious?"

To ask this question is to "speak against" Him as grievously as it would be to ask a good mother if she had forgotten her child. And yet the Lord Himself says: "Can a woman forget her sucking child? Yea, they may forget, yet will I not forget thee." Those of us who are mothers know very well how grieved and insulted we should feel if anyone should suggest the possibility of our forgetting our children; and we mothers at least, if no one else does, should be able to understand how such questioning must grieve the Lord.

"Is God's mercy clean gone forever?" "Hath God in anger shut up his tender mercies?"

To ask these two questions of a good God is to insult Him. It would be as impossible for His tender mercies to be shut up toward us, or for His mercy to go from us forever, as it would be for the tender mercies of a mother come to an end. The psalmist says: "The Lord is good to all, and his tender mercies are over all his works." In the very nature of things this must be, because He is a good God, and cannot do otherwise.

"Do God's promises fail forevermore?"

There come times in every Christian's life when we are tempted to ask this question. Everything seems to be going wrong, and all God's promises seem to have failed. But if we remember that the Lord is good, we shall see that He would cease to be good if such a thing could be. A man who breaks his promises is looked upon as a dishonorable and untrustworthy man; and a God who could break His, if one could imagine such a thing, would be dishonorable and untrustworthy also. And to ask such a question is to cast a stigma on His goodness, that may well be characterized as "speaking against God." No matter how affairs may look, we may be sure of this, that because God is good no promise of His has ever failed, or can ever fail. Heaven and earth may pass away, but His Word never.

"O God, why hast thou cast us off forever?"

It will be impossible for a good God to cast us off as it would be for a good mother to cast off her child. We may be in trouble and darkness, and may feel as if we were cast off and forsaken, but our feelings have nothing to do with the facts, and the fact is that God is good, and could not do it. The good Shepherd does not cast off the sheep that is lost, and take no further care of it, but He goes out to seek for it, and He seeks until He finds it. To suspect Him of casting us off forever is to wound and grieve His faithful love, just as it would wound a good mother's heart is she should be supposed capable of casting off her child, let that child have wandered as far as it may. The thing is impossible in either case, but far more impossible in the case of God than even in the case of the best mother that ever lived.

"Why hast thou made me thus?"

This is a question we are very apt to ask. There is, I imagine, hardly one of us who has not been tempted at one time or another to "reply against God" in reference to the matter of our own personal make-up. We do not like our peculiar temperaments or our especial characteristics, and we long to be like someone else who has, we think, greater gifts of appearance or of talent. We are discontented with our make-up, both inward and outward, and we feel sure that all our failures are because of our unfortunate temperaments; and we are inclined to blame our Creator for having "made us thus."

I remember vividly a time in my life when I was tempted to be very rebellious about my own make-up. I was a plain-spoken, energetic sort of an individual, trying to be a good Christian, but with no especial air of piety about me. But I had a sister who was so saintly in her looks, and had such a pious manner, that she seemed to be the embodiment of piety; and I felt sure I could be a great deal better Christian if only I could get her saintly looks and manner. But all my struggles to get them were useless. My natural temperament was far too energetic and outspoken for any appearance of saintliness, and many a time I said upbraidingly in my heart to God, "Why hast thou made me thus?" But one day I came across a sentence in an old mystic book that seemed to open my eyes. It was as follows: "Be content to be what thy God has made thee"; and it flashed on me that it really was a fact that God had made me, and that He must know the sort of creature He wanted me to be; and that if He had made me a potato vine, I must be satisfied to grow potatoes, and must not want to be a rosebush and grow roses; and if He had fashioned me for humble tasks, I must be content to let others do the grander work. We are "God's workmanship," and God is good, therefore His workmanship must be good also; and we may securely trust that before He is done with us, He will make out of us something that will be to His glory, no matter how unlike this we may as yet feel ourselves to be.

The psalmist seemed to delight in repeating over and over again this blessed refrain, "for the Lord is good." It would be worth while for you to take your concordances and see how often he says it. And he exhorted everyone to join him in saying it. "Let the redeemed of the Lord say so," was his earnest cry. We must join our voices to his—The Lord is good—The Lord is good. But we must not say it with our lips only, and then by our actions give the lie to our words. We must "say" it with our whole being, with thought, word, and action, so that people will see we really mean it, and will be convinced that it is a tremendous fact.

A great many things in God's divine providences do not look like goodness to the eye of sense, and in reading the Psalms we wonder perhaps how the psalmist could say, after some of the things he records, "for his mercy endureth forever." But faith sits down before mysteries such as these, and says, "The Lord is good, therefore all that He does must be good, no matter how it looks, and I can wait for His explanations."

A housekeeping illustration has often helped me here. If I have a friend whom I know to be a good housekeeper, I do not trouble over the fact that at housecleaning time things in her house may seem to be more or less upset, carpets up, and furniture shrouded in coverings, and even perhaps painting and decorating making some rooms uninhabitable. I say to myself, “My friend is a good housekeeper, and although things look so uncomfortable now, all this upset is only because she means in the end to make it far more comfortable than ever it was before.” This world is God’s housekeeping; and although things at present look grievously upset, yet, since we know that He is good, and therefore must be a good Housekeeper, we may be perfectly sure that all this present upset is only to bring about in the end a far better state of things than could have been without it. I dare say we have all felt at times as though we could have done God’s housekeeping better than He does it Himself, but, when we realize that God is good, we can feel this no longer. And it comforts me enormously, when the world seems to me to be going all wrong, just to say to myself, “It is not my housekeeping, but it is the Lord’s; and the Lord is good, therefore His housekeeping must be good too; and it is foolish for me to trouble.”

A deeply taught Christian was asked by a despairing child of God, “Does not the world look to you like a wreck?

“Yes,” was the reply, in a tone of cheerful confidence; “yes, like the wreck of a bursting seed.” Any of us who have watched the first sproutings of an oak tree from the heart of a decaying acorn will understand what this means. Before the acorn can bring forth the oak, it must become itself a wreck. No plant ever came from any but a wrecked seed.

Our Lord uses this fact to teach us the meaning of His processes with us. “Verily, verily, I say unto you, Except a corn of wheat fall into the ground and die, it abideth alone: but, if it die, it bringeth forth much fruit.”

The whole explanation of the apparent wreckage of the world at large, or of our own personal lives in particular, is here set forth. And, looked at in this light, we can understand how it is that the Lord can be good, and yet can permit the existence of sorrow and wrong in the world He has created, and in the lives of the human beings He loves.

It is His very goodness that compels Him to permit it. For He knows that, only through such apparent wreckage, can the fruition of His glorious purposes for us be brought to pass. And we whose hearts also long for that fruition will, if we understand His ways, be able to praise Him for all His goodness, even when things seem hardest and most mysterious.

The apostle tells us that the will of God is “good and acceptable, and perfect.” The will of a good God cannot help being “good”—in fact, it must be perfect’; and, when we come to know this, we always find it “acceptable”; that is we come to love it. I am convinced that all trouble about submitting to the will of God would disappear, if once we could see clearly that His will is good. We struggle and struggle in vain to submit to a will that we do not believe to be good, but when we see that it is really good, we submit to it with delight. We want it to be accomplished. Our hearts spring out to meet it.

*I worship thee, sweet Will of God!*

*And all thy ways adore;*

*And, every day I live, I seem*

*To love thee more and more.*

*I love to kiss each print where thou*

*Hast set thine unseen feet:*

*I cannot fear thee, blessed Will!*

*Thine empire is so sweet.*

Space fails me to tell all that I might of the infinite goodness of the Lord. Each one must "taste and see" for himself. And if he will but do it honestly and faithfully, the words of the psalmist will become true of him: "They shall abundantly utter the memory of thy great goodness, and shall sing of thy righteousness."

# Chapter Eight - The Lord Our Dwelling Place

"Lord, thou hast been our dwelling place in all generations."

The comfort or discomfort of our outward lives depends more largely upon the dwelling place of our bodies than upon almost any other material thing; and the comfort or discomfort of our inward life depends similarly upon the dwelling place of our souls.

Our dwelling place is the place where we live, and not the place we merely visit. It is our home. All the interests of our earthly lives are bound up in our home; and we do all we can to make them attractive and comfortable. But our souls need a comfortable dwelling place even more than our bodies; inward comfort, as we all know, is of far greater importance than outward; and, where the soul is full of peace and joy, outward surroundings are of comparatively little account.

It is of vital importance, then, that we should find out definitely where our souls are living. The Lord declares that He has been our dwelling place in all generations, but the question is, Are we living in our dwelling place? The psalmist says of the children of Israel that "they wandered in the wilderness, in a solitary way; they found no city to dwell in. Hungry and thirsty, their soul fainted in them." And I am afraid there are many wandering souls in the church of Christ, whom this description of the wandering Israelites would exactly fit. All their Christian lives they have been wandering in a spiritual wilderness, and have found no city to dwell in, and, hungry and thirsty, their souls have fainted in them. And yet all the while the dwelling place of God has been standing wide open, inviting them to come in and take up their abode there forever. Out Lord Himself urges this invitation upon us. "Abide in me," He says, "and I in you"; and He goes on to tell us what are the blessed results of this abiding, and what are the sad consequences of not abiding.

The truth is, our souls are made for God. He is our natural home, and we can never be at rest anywhere else. "My soul longeth, yea, even fainteth for the courts of the Lord; my heart and my flesh crieth out for the living God." We always shall hunger and faint for the courts of the Lord, as long as we fail to take up our abode there.

God only is the creature's home; Though rough and straight the road, Yet nothing else can satisfy The soul that longs for God.

How shall we describe this living dwelling place? David describes it when he says: "The Lord is my rock, and my fortress, and my deliverer; the God of my rock; in him will I trust; he is my shield, and the horn of my salvation, my high tower, and my refuge, my Saviour; thou savest me from violence."

So we see that our dwelling place is also our fortress, and our high tower, and our rock, and our refuge. We all know what a fortress is. It is a place of safety, where everything that is weak and helpless can be hidden from the enemy and kept in security. And when we are told that God, who is our dwelling place, is also our fortress, it can mean only one thing, and that is, that if we will but live in our dwelling place, we shall be perfectly safe and secure from every assault of every possible enemy that can attack us. "For in the time of trouble he shall hide me in his pavilion; in the secret of his tabernacle shall he hide me; he shall set me up upon a rock." "He that dwelleth in the secret place of the most High, shall abide under the shadow of the Almighty." "Thou shalt hide them in the secret of thy presence from the pride of man; thou shalt keep them secretly in a pavilion from the strife of tongues."

In the "secret of God's tabernacle" no enemy can find us, and no troubles can reach us. The "pride of man" and the "strife of tongues" find no entrance into the "pavilion" of God. The "secret of his presence" is a more secure refuge than a thousand Gibraltars. I do not mean that no trials come. They may come in abundance, but they cannot penetrate into the sanctuary of the soul, and we may dwell in perfect peace even in the midst of life's fiercest storms.

But alas! how few of us know this. We use David's language, it may be, but to us it is only a figure of speech that has no reality in it. We say the things he said, in the conventional, pious tone that is considered proper when speaking of religious matters. "Oh, yes, the Lord is my dwelling place I know, and I have committed myself and all my interests to His keeping, as of course every Christian ought to do. But"—and here one's natural tones are resumed—"but then I cannot forget that I am a poor good-for-nothing sort of person, and have no strength to conquer my temptations; and I can hardly expect that I can be kept in the perfect security David speaks of." And here will follow a story of all sorts of fears, and anxieties, exactly as if the dwelling place of god had never been heard of, and as if the soul was wandering alone and unprotected in a world of trouble and danger.

There is a psalm that I call the "Dwelling Place of God." It is the Ninety-first Psalm, and it gives us a wonderful description of what this dwelling place is. "He that dwelleth in the secret place of the most High shall abide under the shadow of the Almighty. I will say of the Lord, he is my refuge and my fortress; my God; in him will I trust." Our idea of a fortress is generally of a hard, granite building, where one would be safe, perhaps, but also at the same time sadly uncomfortable. But there are other sorts of fortresses that are soft, and tender, and full of comfort; and this psalm describes them. "He shall cover thee with his feathers," just as the mother hen covers her little helpless chickens in the fortress of her warm, brooking wings. The fortress of a mother's heart, whether it be of a human mother, or a hen mother, or a tiger mother, is the most impregnable fortress the world knows, and yet the tenderest. And it is this sort of a fortress that the Lord is. "Under his wings shalt thou trust": "He shall carry them in his bosom"; "underneath are the everlasting arms."

Wings, bosom, arms! What blessed fortresses are these! And how safe is everything enfolded by them. Nature is full of such fortresses. Listen to what a late writer says of the tiger mother. "When her children are born, some power teaches the tiger to be gentle. A spirit she cannot resist, for it is the spirit of her Creator, enters her savage heart. It is a tiger's impulse to resent an injury. Pluck her by the hair, smite her on the flank, she will leap upon and rend you. But to resent an injury is not her strongest impulse. Watch those impotent kitten creatures playing with her. They are so weak, a careless movement of her giant paw will destroy them; but she makes no careless movement. They have caused her a hundredfold the pain your blow produced; yet she does not render evil for evil. These puny mites of helpless impotence she strokes with love's light in her eyes; she licks the shapeless forms of her tormentors, and, as they plunge at her, love transforms each groan of her anguish into a whinny of delight. She moves her massive head in a way which shows that He who bade you turn the other cheek created her. When strong enough to rise, the terrible creature goes forth to sacrifice herself for her own. She will starve that they may thrive. She is terrible for her little ones, as God is terrible for His."

We have all seen these mother fortresses hundreds of times, and have called them Godlike. And one would think that the sight would have made us fly to our refuge in the dwelling place of God, and leave outside all fear! But the trouble is, we point-blank refuse to believe that the Bible means any such good news. Not in words, perhaps, but in effect, we say, "The Lord's arms are not so dependable as the strong, loving arms of the weakest earthly mother; the Lord's bosom is not as tender as the tiger's bosom; the Lord's wings are not as brooding as the wings of the little mother hen. We know that all these beautiful earthly fortresses are made and fashioned by Him, but we cannot believe that He Himself is equal to them. To have Him for our fortress does not really mean to us anything half so safe or half so tender as to have a mother for our fortress." And so mothers are trusted, and God is not!

And yet how safe the psalmist declares this divine dwelling place to be! Notice how he says, that we who are in this dwelling place shall be afraid of nothing; not for the terror by night, nor the arrow by day, nor for the pestilence that walketh in darkness, nor for the destruction that wasteth at noonday; thousands shall fall beside us and around us, but no evil shall befall the soul that is hidden in this divine dwelling place; no plague shall come nigh those who have made God their "habitation."

All the terrors and all the plagues that have made our religious lives so uncomfortable, an even so wretched, are provided for here, and from all of them we shall be delivered, if we make the Lord our habitation. This does not mean that we shall have no outward trials. Plagues in abundance may attack your body and your goods, but your body and your goods are not yourself; and nothing can come nigh you, the real interior you, while you are dwelling in God.

A large part of the pain of life comes from the haunting "fear of evil" which so often besets us. Our lives are full of supposes. Suppose this should happen, or suppose that should happen; what could we do; how could we bear it? But, if we are living in the "high tower" of the dwelling place of God, all these supposes will drop out of our lives. We shall be "quiet from the fear of evil," for no threatenings of evil can penetrate into the "high tower" of God. Even when walking through the valley of the shadow of death, the psalmist could say, "I will fear no evil"; and, if we are dwelling in God, we can say so too.

But you may ask here how you are to get into this divine dwelling place. To this I answer that you must simply move in. If a house should be taken for us by a friend, and we were told it was ready, and that the lease and all the necessary papers were duly attested and signed, we should not ask how we could get into it—we should just pack up and move in. And we must do the same here. God says that He is our dwelling place, and the Bible contains all the necessary papers, duly attested and signed. And our Lord invites us, nay more, commands us to enter in and abide there. In effect He says, "God is your dwelling place, and you must see to it that you take up your abode there. You must move in."

But how, you ask, how can I move in? You must do it by faith. God has said that He is your dwelling place, and now you must say it too. "I will say of the Lord, he is my refuge and my fortress: my God; in him will I trust." Faith takes up the Word of God, and asserts it to be true. Christ says, "Abide," and we must say, "I will abide." Thus we "make him our habitation" by faith. He is our habitation already, as to His side of it; but we must make Him so, as to our side of it, by believing that He is, and by continually asserting it. Coleridge says:

Faith is an affirmation and an act, That bids eternal truth be present fact.

And we must make the eternal truth that the Lord is our dwelling place become present fact by the affirmation of our faith, and by putting on the thoughts and actions that would naturally result from having moved into the tabernacle of God.

And one of the first things we would have to do would be to give up forever all worry and anxiety. It is unthinkable that worry and anxiety could enter into the dwelling place of God; and when we enter there, we must leave them behind.

We talk about obeying the commands of the Lord, and make a great point of outward observances and outward duties, and all the while neglect and ignore the commands as to the inward life, which are a thousandfold more important. "Let not your heart be troubled, neither let it be afraid," is one of our Lord's commands that is almost universally disobeyed; and yet I question whether our disobedience of any other command is so grievous to His heart. I am very sure for myself, that I would be far more grieved if my child should mistrust me, and should feel her interests were unsafe in my care, than if in a moment of temptation she should disobey me. And I am convinced that none of us have appreciated how deeply it wounds the loving heart of our Lord, when He finds that His people do not feel safe in His care.

We can know this by ourselves. Suppose one of our friends should commit something to our keeping, receiving from us every assurance that we would keep it safe, and then should go away and worry over it, as we worry over the things we commit to God, and should express to others the anxieties about it that we allow ourselves to express about the things we have put into God's care. How, I would like to know, would we feel about it? Would we not be deeply hurt and wounded; and would we not finally be inclined to hand the thing back into our friend's own care, and to say, "Since it is very plain that you do not trust me, had you not better take care of your things yourself?" It is amazing that God's own children can dare to be anxious, after once they have committed a matter to Him; it is such a libel on His trustworthiness. And of course outsiders judge it in this way, and think to themselves that to have the Lord for your dwelling place does not evidently amount to much after all, or those who profess to be living there could not be so troubled.

He who cares for the sparrows, and numbers the hairs of our head, cannot possibly fail us. He is an impregnable fortress into which no evil can enter and no enemy penetrate. I hold it, therefore, as a self-evident truth that the moment I have really committed anything into this divine dwelling place, that moment all fear and anxiety should cease. While I keep anything in my own care, I may well fear and tremble, for it is indeed to the last degree unsafe; but in God's care, no security could be more absolute.

The psalmist says: "The name of the Lord is a strong tower: the righteous runneth into it, and is safe." The only point, therefore, is to "run into" this strong tower and stay there forever. It would be the height of folly, when the enemy was surrounding us on every side to stand outside of a fortress and cry out for safety. If I want to be safe, I must go in.

"O Jerusalem, Jerusalem!" said our Lord, "thou that killest the prophets, and stonest them which are sent unto thee, how often would I have gathered thy children together, even as a hen gathereth her chickens under her wings, and ye would not." If the little children wants to be safe, it must "run into" the fortress of its mother's wings. A great many people stay outside of God's dwelling place, because they feel themselves too unworthy and too weak to dare to go in. What would we think of the little chicken that would see the hawk coming, would hear the mother calling, and see her outspread wings, but would stand outside, trembling with fright, saying, "Oh, I am such a poor, weak, foolish, helpless little chicken that I am afraid I am not worthy to go under my mother's wings"? If the mother hen could speak, I am sure she would say, "You poor, foolish little thing, it is just because you are weak, and helpless, and good for nothing, that I want you under my wings. If you were a great, big, strong rooster, able to take care of yourself, I would not want you at all." Need I make the application?

But we must not only "run into" our dwelling place. The psalmist says: "I will abide in thy tabernacle forever: I will trust in the covert of thy wings"; and we must do the same. This "abiding in his tabernacle forever" is, I am free to confess, sometimes very hard. It is comparatively easy to take a step of faith, but it is a far more difficult thing to abide steadfastly in the place into which we have stepped. A great many people "run into" God's fortress on Sunday, and come out of it again as soon as Monday morning dawns. Some even run into it when they kneel down to say their prayers at night, and come out of it five minutes afterward when they get into bed. Of course, this is the height of folly. One cannot imagine any sensible refugee running into a fortress one day, and the next day running out among the enemy again. We should think such a person had suddenly lost all his senses. But is it not even more foolish when it comes to the soul? Are our enemies any less active on Mondays than they are on Sundays, or are we any better able to cope with them when we are in bed than when we were kneeling at our prayers?

The question is, Do we want to pay visits only to the dwelling place of God, or do we want to live there? Do we want to "trust in the covert of his wings" today, and tomorrow be exposed to the buffetings of our enemies outside? No one would deliberately choose the latter, but far too many drift into it. Our abiding in Christ is altogether a matter of faith, but we fail to realize this. We think our earnest wrestlings or our strenuous efforts are a large part of the matter; and, when these slacken, our faith weakens. But if there is one thing more certain than another, it is that the whole Christian life is to be lived by faith. Without faith it is impossible to please God; and it is perfect folly to fancy that any amount of fervency or earnestness or anything whatever of our own doing can take its place; and it is manifestly useless to waste our time and energy over things that amount to nothing.

What we must do is to put all our will power and all our energy into faith. We must "set our faces like a flint" to move into the dwelling place of God, and to abide there steadfastly, let the temptations to doubt or discouragement be what they may.

"He that dwelleth in the secret place of the most High shall abide under the shadow of the Almighty. Abiding and trusting are synonymous words, and mean exactly the same thing. While I trust the Lord, I am abiding in Him. If I trust Him steadfastly, I am abiding in Him steadfastly; if I trust Him intermittently, I am running into Him and running out again. I used to think there was some mystery about abiding in Christ, but I see now that it only means trusting Him fully. When once you understand this, it becomes really the simplest matter in the world. We sometimes say, speaking of two human beings, that they "live in each other's hearts," and we simply mean that perfect love and confidence exists between them, and that doubts of one another are impossible. If my trust in the fortress of the Lord is absolute, I am abiding in that fortress; and this is the whole story.

The practical thing to do, therefore, in face of the fact that God is declared to be our fortress and our high tower, is, by a definite act of surrender and faith, to put ourselves and all our interests of every kind into this divine dwelling place, and then dismiss all care or anxiety about them from our minds. Since the Lord is our dwelling place, nothing can possibly come to any harm that is committed to His care. As long as we believe this, our affairs remain in His care; the moment we begin to doubt, we take our affairs into our own hands, and they are no longer in the divine fortress. Things cannot be in two places at once. If they are in our own care, they cannot be in God's care; and if they are in God's care, they cannot be in our own. This is as clear as daylight, and yet, for the want of a little common sense, people often get mixed up over it. They put their affairs into God's fortress, and at the same time put them into their own fortress as well, and then wonder why they are not taken care of. This is all folly. Either trust the Lord out and out, or else trust yourself out and out; but do not try to mix the two trusts, for they will not mix.

It will help you practically if you will put your trust into words. Say definitely, "God is my dwelling place, and I am going to abide in Him forever. It is all settled; I am in this divine habitation, and I am safe here, and I am not going to move out again." You must meet all assaults of doubt and discouragement with the simple assertion that you are there, and that you know you will not be confounded; let other people do as they may, but you must declare that you at any rate are going to abide in your divine dwelling place forever. And then, having taken this stand, you must utterly refuse to reconsider the matter. It is all settled; and there is nothing more to be said about it.

In all this I do not, or course, mean that we are to lie in bed and let things go. I am talking about the inward aspect of our affairs, not the outward. Outwardly we may have to be full of active carefulness, but it must all be from the inward basis of a soul that has hidden itself and all its interests in the dwelling place of God, and that is therefore "careful for nothing" in the beautiful Bible sense of having no anxious thoughts. To be thus without care inwardly is the surest foundation for successful outward care; and the soul that is hidden in the dwelling place of

God is the soul that will be able to bear triumphantly earth's greatest trials, and to conquer its strongest foes.

There is one point I must not fail to mention. When we move into a new house, we not only move in ourselves, but we take with us all our belongings of every sort or description, and above all we take our family. No one would be so foolish as to leave anything he cared for or anyone he loved outside. But I am afraid there are some of God's children, who move into the dwelling place of God themselves, but who, by their lack of faith, leave outside those they love best; and more often than not it is their children who are so abandoned. We would be horrified at a father who, in a time of danger, should flee into a fortress for safety, but should leave his children outside; and yet hundreds of Christians do this very thing. Every anxious thought in which we indulge about our children proves that we have not really taken them with us into the dwelling place of God.

What I mean is this, that if we trust for ourselves, we must trust for our loved ones also, and especially for our children. God is more their Father than their earthly fathers are and if they are dear to us, they are far dearer to Him. We cannot, therefore, do anything better for them than to trust them to His care, and hardly anything worse than to try to keep them in our own. I knew a Christian mother who trusted peacefully for her own salvation, but was racked with anxiety about her sons, who seemed entirely indifferent to all religious subjects. One evening she heard about the possibility of putting those we love into the fortress of God by faith and leaving them there; and, like a flash of heavenly light, she saw the inconsistency of hiding herself in God's fortress and leaving her beloved sons outside. At once her faith took them into the fortress with her, and she abandoned them to the care of God. So fully and completely did she do this that all her anxiety vanished, and perfect peace dawned upon her soul. She told me she felt somehow that her sons were God's sons now—no longer hers—and that He loved them far better than she could, and would care for them far more wisely and effectually. She held herself in readiness to do for them whatever the Lord might suggest; but she felt that He was the One who would know what was best, and she was content to leave the matter in His hands.

She went home from that meeting and called her sons into her room, telling them what had happened; she said, "You know, my dear boys, how anxious and troubled I have been about you, and how continually I have preached to you, and I am afraid have often worried you. But now I have learned to trust, and I have put you by faith into the fortress of God, and have left you in His care. I am sure that He will care for you far better than your poor mother ever could, and will save you in His own way. My anxieties are over."

I did not see her again for a year, but when I did, she came up to me with a beaming face; and with tears of joy filling her eyes, she said, "Rejoice with me, dear friend, that I learned how to put my boys into the fortress of God. They have been safe there ever since, and all of them are good Christian boys today."

The conclusion of the whole matter, then, is simply this, that we must make up our minds to move into our dwelling place in God and to take there with us all our possessions, above all, those we love. We must hide ourselves in Him away from ourselves, away from all others, and we must lose sight of everything that is outside of Him except as we see it through His eyes. God's eyes are the windows of God's house, and the only windows there are; and seen through His eyes, all things will put on a new aspect. We shall see our trials as blessings, and our enemies as disguised friends. We shall be calm and at rest in the face of all the frets and worries of life, untouched by any of them. "For he that dwelleth in God dwelleth in a peaceable habitation and in a quiet resting place."

# Chapter Nine - Much More Versus Much Less

"But where sin abounded grace did much more abound."

In our preceding chapters we have been trying to learn something about the Lord and His great salvation; and now the vital point is, what view do we take of it all? A very great deal of the comfort or discomfort of our religious lives depends on the view we take of things. I do not mean of course that our view of things affects their reality in any way, but what I do mean is that our view makes all the difference in our apprehension of this reality; and while our safety comes from what things really are, our comfort comes from what we suppose them to be.

There is an expression used over and over again in the Bible to describe the salvation of the Lord Jesus Christ, which gives a view of that salvation, so amazing and so perfectly satisfying, that I cannot help wondering whether any of us have ever yet grasped its full meaning. One thing is certain, that no one who grasps it could ever be uncomfortable or miserable again. It is the expression, "much more," and it is used to tell us, if only we would believe it, that there is no need which any human being can ever know that cannot be much more than met by the glorious salvation that is provided. But we are continually tempted to think that much less would be a truer term; and that, so far from this salvation being much more than our needs, it turns out in actual experience to be much less. And this "much less" view, if I may so express it, is in danger of making our whole spiritual lives a misery to us.

If all we have been learning in our preceding chapters of the fullness of God's salvation is indeed true, it would seem as if nothing but the language of "much more" could ever be used by any child of God. But since there are some Christians, who seem by their thoughts and their actions to declare that they consider the language of "much less" to be the only prudent language for poor sinners, I want us carefully to consider the matter in the light of what the Bible tells us, and discover whether we are really justified in saying much more.

It is, I believe, a far more vital question for each one of us than may appear at first sight. For if God declares that the salvation He has provided is much more than enough to meet our needs, and if we insist on declaring in our secret thoughts that it is much less, we are casting discredit on His trustworthiness, and are storing up for ourselves untold discomfort and misery.

"Much less" is the language of the seen thing, "much more" is the language of the unseen thing. "Much less" seems on the surface to be far more reasonable than "much more," because every seen thing confirms it. Our weakness and foolishness are visible; God's strength and wisdom are invisible. Our need is patent before our very eyes; God's supply is hidden in the secret of His presence, and can only be realized by faith.

It seems a paradox to tell us that we must see unseen things. How can it be possible? But there are other things to see than those which appear on surfaces, and other eyes to look through than those we generally use. An ox and a scientist may both look at the same field, but they will see very different things there. To see unseen things requires us to have that interior eye opened in our souls which is able to see below surfaces, and which can pierce through the outer appearance of things into their inner realities. This interior eye looks not at the seen things, which are temporal, but at the things that are not seen, which are eternal; and the vital question for each one of us is, whether that interior eye has been opened in us yet, and whether we can see the things that are eternal, or whether our vision is limited to the things that are temporal only.

Can and do we say of the salvation of the Lord Jesus Christ that it is much more than our need, or that it is much less?

There is a wonderful instance in the history of the children of Israel, when they saw the unseen things with such clearness of vision, that the "much less" of their enemy, and of the seen things around them, was powerless to disturb them. The story is told in II Chronicles 32:1-15. An enemy had come up against Judah, and had threatened to overwhelm them. This enemy had been so universally successful hitherto in all his wars with the nations round about that he had no doubt he would be able to conquer the Israelites also. But Hezekiah, the king of Israel, looked not at the seen enemy, but at the unseen God, and he saw that God was the strongest; and he spake comfortable to the people, and said: "Be strong and courageous, be not afraid nor dismayed for the king of Assyria, nor for all the multitude that is with him; for there be more with us than with him. With him is an arm of flesh; but with us is the Lord our God, to help us, and to fight our battles." What a tremendous contrast: on one side an arm of flesh; on the other, the Lord our God! No wonder the people "rested themselves" upon a declaration such as this.

And yet, I cannot help questioning whether if we had been there, we would have had faith enough to have so rested ourselves?

When Sennacherib saw their faith, he was enraged, and upbraided them with this folly in being persuaded by Hezekiah to expose themselves to the risk of death by thirst and famine in the vain hope that the Lord would deliver them. And then comes the taunt of the "much less": "Know you not," he said, "what I and my father have done unto all the people of other lands? Were the gods of the nations of those lands in any way able to deliver their lands out of mine hand? Who was there among all the gods of those nations that could deliver his people out of mine hand, that your God shall be able to deliver you out mine hand? Now therefore let not Hezekiah deceive you, nor persuade you on this manner, neither yet believe him; for no god of any nation or kingdom was able to deliver his people out of mine hand, how much less shall your God deliver you out of mine hand."

"How much less"—what a temptation to unbelief was contained in those words! All the seen things were on that side; and it did look impossible, in the face of the fact that all the nations round about had been defeated, that the nation of Israel, no stronger, and no better equipped than the others, should find deliverance. But Hezekiah kept his eyes and the eyes of the people fixed on the unseen things, and their faith stood firm; and the Lord in whom they trusted did not fail them, but sent them a grand deliverance. The "much less" of the enemy was turned for the Israelites into a "much more" of victory. The man who had promised them defeat and death was himself defeated; he was obliged to return to his own land with "shame of face," and was there slain by his disappointed relatives.

Is there nothing analogous to this story in our own personal history? Have we never been taunted with the discouraging thought that God is "much less" able to deliver us than His promises would lead us to expect? And when we have looked at the formidable seen things of our need has it not sometimes seemed to us as if it would be equivalent to giving ourselves over to "die by famine and thirst," if we were brought to the point of having absolutely nothing else to trust to but the Lord alone? I remember hearing of a Christian who was in great trouble, and who had tried every way for deliverance, but in vain, who said finally to another in a tone of the utmost despair, "Well, there is nothing left for me now but to trust the Lord."

"Alas!" exclaimed the friend in the greatest consternation, "is it possible it has come to that?"

We may shrink with horror from the thought of using such an expression, but, if we are honest with ourselves, I believe we shall be obliged to confess that sometimes, in the very bottom of our hearts, we have indulged in just this feeling. To come to the point of having nothing left to trust in but the Lord has, I am afraid, seemed to us at times a desperate condition of things. And yet, if our Lord is to be believed, His "much mores" of grace are abundantly equal to the worst emergency that can befall us. The apostle tells us that God is able to do "exceeding abundantly above all that we can ask or think"; and this describes what His "much mores" mean. We can think of very wonderful things in the way of salvation—spiritual blessing that would transform life for us, and make the whole universe resplendent with joy and triumph—and we can ask for them. But do we really believe that God is able and willing to do for us "exceeding abundantly" above all that we can ask or think? Is the language of our hearts "much more" or "much less"?

In another place we are told that "eye hath not seen, nor ear heard, neither have entered into the heart of man, the things which God hath prepared for them that love him." If God has prepared more for us than it has ever entered into our hearts to conceive, surely we can have no question about obtaining that which has entered into our hearts, and "much more" beside. What can it be then but downright unbelief that leads any of us to harbor a thought of God's salvation being "much less" than the things it has entered into our hearts to long for.

Let us settle it then that the language of our souls must henceforth be not the "much less" of unbelief, but the "much more" of faith. And I feel sure we shall find that God's "much mores" will be enough to cover the whole range of our needs, both temporal and spiritual.

"For if through the offense of one many be dead, much more the grace of God and the gift by grace which is by one man, Jesus Christ, hath abounded unto man." This is a "much more" that really reaches, if only we could understand it, into the deepest depth of human need. There is no question in our minds as to the fact that "many be dead," but how is it with the "much more" of grace that is to abound unto many? Are we sure of the grace that is to abound unto many? Are we as sure of the grace as we are of the death? Do we really believe that the remedy is "much more" than the disease? Does the salvation seem to us "much more" than the need? Or do we believe in our hearts that it is "much less"? Which does God declare?

One of the deepest needs of our souls is the need for being saved. Is there a "much more" to meet this need? What does the apostle say? "But God commendeth his love toward us, in that, while we were yet sinners, Christ died for us. Much more then, being now justified by his blood, we shall be saved from wrath through him. For if, when we were enemies, we were reconciled to God by the death of his Son, much more, being reconciled, we shall be saved by his life." The question of salvation seems to me to be absolutely settled by these "much mores." Since Christ has died for us, and has thereby reconciled us to God (not God to us, He did not need reconciling), of course "much more," if only we will let Him, will He now save us. There can be no question as to whether He will save us. There can be no question as to whether He will or will not, for the greater must necessarily include the lesser, and, having done the greater, "much more" will He do the lesser. We none of us doubt that He did the greater, and, in the face of these "much mores," we dare not doubt He will do the lesser.

Now the practical point for us in all this is, Do we really believe it? Have we got rid of all doubts as to our salvation? Can we speak with assurance of forgiveness and of eternal life? Do we say with the timidity of unbelief, "I hope I am a child of

God"; or do we lift up our heads, with joyous confidence in God as our Father, and say with John, "Now are we the sons of God"? Is it in this respect "much more" with us, or "much less"?

We long and pray for the gift of the Holy Spirit, but it seems all in vain. We feel that our prayers are not answered. But our Lord gives faith a wonderful "much more" to lay hold of for this. "If ye then, being evil, know how to give good gifts unto your children, how much more shall your heavenly Father give the Holy Spirit to them that ask him?" There is not one of us who does not know how thankful and eager good parents are to give good gifts to their children—how they thrust them on the children often before the child is ready to receive, or even knows that it has a need. And yet, who of us really believes that God is actually "much more" eager to give the Holy Spirit to them that ask Him? Is it not rather that many feel secretly that He is "much less" willing, and that we will have to beg, and entreat, and wrestle, and wait, for this sorely needed gift? If we could only believe this "much more," how full of faith our asking would be in regard to it. We should then truly be able to believe that we actually did receive that for which we had asked, and should find that we were in actual possession of the Holy Spirit as our present and personal Comforter and Guide; and all our weary struggles and agonizing prayers for this promised gift would be over.

Sorer, perhaps, than any other need is our need of victory over sin and over circumstances. Like Juggernaut cars they roll over us with irresistible power, and crush us into the dust. And the language of "much less" seems the only language that our souls dare utter. But God has given us for this a most triumphant "much more." "For, if by one man's offense, death reigned by one, much more they which receive abundance of grace, and of the gift of righteousness, shall reign in life by one, Jesus Christ."

We have known the reigning of that spiritual death which comes by sin, and have groaned under its power. But how much do we know of that "much more" reigning in life by Jesus Christ of which the apostle speaks? That is, have we now greater victories than we used to have defeats? Do we reign over things "much more" than they once reigned over us?

I mean this, that in the Gospel it is promised that we shall be "more than conquerors" over the very things that once conquered us, and the question is whether we really are. We have been reigned over by thousands of things, by the fear of man, by our peculiar temperaments, by our outward circumstances, by our irritable tempers, even by bad weather, by our environment of every kind. We have been slaves where we ought to have been kings. We have found our reigning to be "much less" rather than "much more." Why is this? Simply because we have not "received" enough of the abundance of grace that is ours in Christ. We have let unbelief cheat us out of our rightful possessions. We are called to be kings and are "made to have dominion," but here God declares that it shall be "much more" of a dominion than it was formerly a bondage; have we so found it? If not, why not? The lack cannot possibly be on God's side. He has not failed to provide the "much more" of victory. It must be that we have in some way failed to avail ourselves of it. And I cannot but believe that our failure arises from the fact that we have substituted our "much less" for God's "much more"; and in our heart of hearts have not believed there really is a sufficiency in the gift of righteousness in Christ to enable us to reign. We have failed through our unbelief to "receive the abundance of grace" that is necessary for reigning.

What then is our remedy? Only this—to abandon forever our "much less" of unbelief, and to accept as true God's declaration of "much more," and to claim at once the promised victory. And according to our faith it must and will be unto us.

But these assurances of the "much mores" of God's salvation are not for our spiritual needs only, but for our temporal needs as well. Do not be anxious, He says, about earthly things, for "if God so clothe the grass of the field, which today is, and tomorrow is cast into the oven, shall he not much more clothe you, O ye of little faith?"

I know that to many Christians this passage and others like it are so familiar that they have almost lost all meaning. But they do mean something, and something almost too wonderful for belief. They tell us that God cares for us human beings "much more" than He cares for the universe around us, and that He will watch over and provide for us much more than He will even for it.

Incredible, yet true! How often we have marveled at the orderly working of the universe, and have admired the great creative Power that made it and now controls it! But none of us, I suppose, has ever felt it necessary to take the burden of the universe upon our own shoulders. We have trusted the Creator to manage it all without our help. Although I must confess, from the way some people find fault with the Creator's management of things, and the advice they seem to feel it necessary to give Him in their prayers, one would think the whole burden was resting upon them!

But even where we have fully recognized that the universe is altogether in God's care, we have failed to see that we also are there, and have never dreamed that it could be true that "much more" than He cares for the universe will He care for us. We have looked at the seen things of our circumstances and our surroundings, and at the greatness of our need and our own helplessness, and have been anxious and afraid. We have burdened ourselves with the care of ourselves, feeling in our unbelief that, instead of being of "much more" value than the fowls of the air, or the lilies of the field, we are in reality of infinitely "much less"; and it seems to us that the God who cares for them is not at all likely to care for us. We say with the psalmist: "When I consider thy heavens, the work of thy fingers, the moon and the stars, which thou hast ordained; what is man, that thou art mindful of him? and the son of man that thou visited him?" Man so puny, so insignificant, of so little account when compared with the great, wide universe, what is he, we ask, that God should care for him? And yet God declares that He does care for him, and that He even cares for him much more than He cares for the universe. Much more, remember, not much less. So that every thought of anxiety about ourselves must be immediately crushed with the common-sense reflection that, since we are not so foolish as to be anxious about the universe, we must not be so much more foolish as to be anxious about ourselves.

In the Sermon on the Mount, our Lord gives us the crowning "much more" of all. "Or what man is there of you, whom if his son ask bread, will he give him a stone? Or if he ask a fish, will he give him a serpent? If ye then, being evil, know how to give good gifts unto your children, how much more shall your Father which is in heaven gives good things to them that ask him?"

In this "much more" we have a warrant for the supply of every need. Whatever our Father sees to be good for us is here abundantly promised. And the illustration used to convince us is one of universal application. In all ranks and condition of life, among all nations, and even in the hearts of birds and beasts the mother instinct never fails to provide for its offspring the best it can compass. Under no conditions of life will a mother, unless she is wicked beyond compare, give a stone when asked for bread, or a serpent when asked for fish. And could our God, who created the mother heart, be worse than a mother? No, no, a thousand times no! What He will do is "much more," oh, so much more than even the tenderest mother could do. And if mothers "know how," as surely they do, to give good things to their children, "how much more" does He. But do we really believe this "much more"? Our hours of anxious tossing on our beds must answer. If God is actually much more willing and able to give good things to us than parents are to give good things to their children, then all possibility of doubt or anxiety as to our prayers being answered must vanish forever. All "good things" must be given to us when we ask, as inevitably as the mother who is able feeds her child when it asks her for bread. As inevitably, do I say? Ah, dear friends, far more inevitably. For it is "how much more" shall your Father which is in Heaven. Which of us has fathomed the meaning of this "how much more"? But at least this it must mean, that all human readiness to hear and answer the cry of need can only be a faint picture of God's readiness, and that, therefore, we can never dare to doubt again. And if parents would not give a stone for bread, neither would He; so that when we ask, we must be absolutely sure that we do receive the "good thing" for which we asked, whether what we receive looks like it or not.

The mother of St. Augustine, in her longing for the conversion of her son, prayed that he might not go to Rome, as she feared its dissipations. God answered her by sending him to Rome to be converted there. Things we call good are often God's evil things, and our evil is His good. But, however things may look, we always know that God must give the best because He is God and could do no other.

"He that spared not his own Son, but delivered him up for us all, how shall he not with him also freely give us all things." Since He has done the supreme thing of having given us Christ, "much more" will He do the less by giving us all things with Him. And yet we continually hear God's own children lamenting their spiritual poverty, and their state of spiritual starvation, and even, it seems sometimes, thinking it rather a pious thing to do and a mark of true humility. But what is this but glorying in the "much less" of their unbelief, instead of in the "much more" of God.

"Oh, I am such a poor creature," I heard a child of God say once with actual complacency when urged to some victory of faith; "I am such a poor creature that I cannot expect to attain to the heights you grand Christians reach." "Poor creature," indeed; of course you are, and so are we all! But God is not poor, and it is His part to supply your needs, not your part to supply His. He is able, no matter what unbelief may say, to "make all grace abound toward you, that ye always having all sufficiency in all things may abound to every good work." "All," "always," "every"—what all-embracing words these are! They include our needs to their utmost limit, and leave us no room for any question. How can we, how dare we, in the face of such declarations, ever doubt or question again?

We have only touched upon the wonders of grace hidden in these "much mores" of God. We can never exhaust their meaning in this life. But let us at least resolve henceforth to lay aside every "much less" of unbelief on all the lines of salvation, and out of the depths of our utter weakness, sinfulness, and need assert with a conquering faith always and everywhere the mighty "much more" of the grace of God!

# Chapter Ten - Self-Examination

"Examine yourselves, whether ye be in the faith."

Probably no subject connected with the religious life has been the cause of more discomfort and suffering to tender consciences than has this subject of self-examination; and none has led more frequently to the language of "much less," which we found in our last chapter to be so great an obstacle to all spiritual growth. And yet it has been so constantly impressed upon us that it is our duty to examine ourselves, that the eyes of most of us are continually turned inward, and our gaze is fixed on our own interior states and feelings to such an extent that self, and not Christ, has come at last to fill the whole horizon.

By self I mean here all that centers around this great big "me" of ours. Its vocabulary rings out the changes on "I," "me," "my." It is a vocabulary with which we are all very familiar. The questions we ask ourselves in our times of self-examination are proof of this. Am I earnest enough? Have I repented enough? Have I the right sort of feelings? Do I realize religious truth as I ought? Are my prayers fervent enough? Is my interest in religious things as great as it ought to be? Do I love God with enough fervor? Is the Bible as much of a delight to me as it is to others? All these, and a hundred more questions about ourselves and our experiences fill up all our thoughts, and sometimes our little self-examination books as well; and day and night we ring the changes on the person pronoun "I," "me," "my," to the utter exclusion of any thought concerning Christ, or any word concerning "He," "His," "Him."

The misery of this, many of us know only too well. But the idea that the Bible is full of commands to self-examination is so prevalent that it seems one of the most truly pious things we can do; and, miserable as it makes us, we still feel it is our duty to go on with it in spite of an ever-increasing sense of hopelessness and despair.

In view of this idea many will be surprised to find that there are only two texts in the whole Bible that speak of self-examination, and that neither of these can at all be made to countenance the morbid self-analysis that results from what we call self-examination.

One of these passages I have quoted at the head of this chapter: "Examine yourselves, whether ye be in the faith." This is simply an exhortation to the Corinthians, who were in a sadly backsliding condition, to settle definitely whether they were still believers or not. "Examine yourselves, whether ye be in the faith." It does not say examine whether you are sufficiently earnest, or whether you have the right feelings, or whether your motives are pure, but simply and only, whether you are "in the faith." In short, do you believe in Christ or do you not? A simple question that required only a simple, straightforward answer, Yes or No. This is what it meant for the Corinthians then, and it is what it means for us now.

The other passage reads: "Wherefore, whosoever shall eat this bread and drink this cup of the Lord unworthily, shall be guilty of the body and blood of the Lord. But let a man examine himself, and so let him eat of that bread and drink of that cup." Paul was here writing of the abuses of greediness and drunkenness which had crept in at the celebration of the Lord's Supper; and, in this exhortation to examine themselves, he was simply urging them to see to it that they did none of these things, but partook of this religious feast in a decent and orderly manner.

In neither of these passages is there any hint of that morbid searching out of one's emotions and experiences that is called self-examination in the present day. And it is amazing that out of two such simple passages should have been evolved a teaching fraught with so much misery to earnest, conscientious souls.

The truth is there is no Scripture authority whatever for this disease of modern times; and those who are afflicted with it are the victims of mistaken ideas of God's ways with His children.

Some of my readers, however, are probably asking themselves whether I have not overlooked a large class of passages that tell us to "watch"; and whether these passages do not mean watching ourselves, or, in other words, self-examination. I will quote one of these passages as a sample, that we may see what their meaning really is. "But of that day and that hour knoweth no man, no not the angels which are in heaven, neither the Son, but the Father. Take ye heed, watch and pray; for ye know not when the time is. For the Son of man is as a man taking a far journey, who left his home, and gave authority to his servants, and to every man his work, and commanded the porter to watch. Watch ye therefore, for ye know not when the master of the house cometh, at even, or at midnight, or at the cock-crowing, or in the morning: lest coming suddenly he find you sleeping. And what I say unto you, I say unto all, Watch."

I think if we carefully examine this passage and others like it, we shall see that instead of teaching self-examination, they teach something that is exactly the opposite. They tell us to "watch," it is true, but they do not tell us to watch ourselves. They are plainly commands to forget ourselves in watching for Another. The return of the Lord is the thing we are to watch for. His coming footsteps, and not our own past footsteps, are to be the object of our gazing. We are to watch as a porter watches for the return of the master of the house, and are to be ready as a good watchman should be to receive and welcome Him at any moment that He may appear.

"Blessed are those servants whom the Lord when he cometh shall find watching." Watching what? Themselves? No, watching for Him, of course. If we can imagine a porter, instead of watching for the return of his master, spending his time morbidly analyzing his own past conduct, trying to discover whether he had been faithful enough, and becoming so absorbed in self-examination as to let the master's call go unheeded and the master's return unnoted, we shall have a picture of what goes on in the experience of the soul that is given up to the mistaken habit of watching and looking at self instead of watching and looking for Christ.

These passages, therefore, instead of teaching self-examination, teach exactly the opposite. God says, "Look unto me, and ye shall be saved"; but the self-analyzing soul says, "I must look unto myself, if I am to have any hope of being saved. It must be by getting myself right that salvation is to come." And yet the phrase, "Looking unto Jesus," is generally acknowledged to be one of the watchwords of the Christian religion; and all Christians everywhere will unhesitatingly declare that, or course, this is the one thing we all ought to do. But, after saying this, they will go on in their old way of self-introspection, trying to find some salvation in their own inward feelings, or in their own works of righteousness, and being continually plunged into despair because they never find it.

It is a fact that we see what we look at, and cannot see what we look away from; and we cannot look unto Jesus while we are looking at ourselves. The power for victory and the power for endurance are to come from looking unto Jesus and considering Him, not from looking unto or considering ourselves, or our circumstances, or our sins, or our temptations. Looking at ourselves causes weakness and defeat. The reason for this is that when we look at ourselves, we see nothing but ourselves, and our own weakness, and poverty, and sin; we do not and cannot see the remedy and the supply for these, and as a matter of course we are defeated. The remedy and the supply are there all the time, but they are not to be found in the place where we are looking, for they are not in self but in Christ; and we cannot be looking at ourselves and looking at Christ at the same time. Again I repeat that it is in the inexorable nature of things that what we look at that we shall see, and that, if we want to see the Lord, we must look at the Lord and not at self. It is a simple question of choice for us, whether it shall be I or Christ; whether we shall turn our backs on Christ and look at ourselves, or whether we shall turn our backs on self and look at Christ.

I was very much helped many years ago by the following sentence in a book by Adelaide Proctor: "For one look at self take ten looks at Christ." It was entirely contrary to all I had previously thought right; but it carried conviction to my soul, and delivered me from a habit of morbid self-examination and introspection that had made my life miserable for years. It was an unspeakable deliverance. And my experience since leads me to believe that even a better motto would be, "Take no look at self at all, but look only and always at Christ."

The Bible law in regard to the self-life is not that the self-life must be watched and made better, but that it must be "put off." The apostle, when urging the Ephesian Christians to walk worthy of the vocation wherewith they had been called, tells them that they must "put off" the old man which is corrupt according to the deceitful lusts. The "old man" is, of course, the self-life, and this self-life (which we know only too well is indeed corrupt according to deceitful lusts) is not to be improved, but to be "put off." It is to be crucified. Paul says that our old man is crucified, put to death, with Christ; and he declares of the Colossians that they could no longer lie, seeing that they had "put of the old man with his deeds." Some people's idea of crucifying the "old man" is to set him up on a pinnacle, and then walk around him and stick nagging pins into him to make him miserable, but keeping him alive all the time. But, if I understand language, crucifixion means death, not making miserable; and to crucify the old man means to kill him outright, and to put him off as a snake puts off its dead and useless skin.

It is of no use, then, for us to examine self and to tinker with it in the hope of improving it, for the thing the Lord wants us to do with it is to get rid of it. Fenelon, in his Spiritual Letters, says that the only way to treat self is to refuse to have anything to do with it. He says we must turn our backs on this great big "I" of ours, and to say to it, "I do not know you, and am not interested in you, and I refuse to pay any attention to you whatever." But self is always determined to secure attention, and would rather be thought badly of than not to be thought of at all. And self-examination with all its miseries often gives a sort of morbid satisfaction to the self-life in us, and even deludes self into thinking it a very humble and pious sort of self after all.

The only safe and scriptural way is to have nothing to do with self at all, either with good self or with bad self, but simply to ignore self altogether; and to fix our eyes, and our thoughts, and our expectations on the Lord and on Him alone. We must substitute for the personal pronouns "I," "me," "my," the pronoun "He," "Him," "His"; and must ask ourselves, not "am I good?" but "is He good?"

The psalmist says: "Mine eyes are ever toward the Lord, for he shall pluck my feet out of the net." As long as our eyes are toward our own feet, and toward the net in which they are entangled, we only get into worse tangles. But when we keep our eyes toward the Lord, He plucks our feet out of the net. This is a point in practical experience that I have tested hundreds of times, and I know it is a fact. No matter what sort of a snarl I may have been in, whether inward or outward, I have always found that while I kept my eyes on the snarl and tried to unravel it, it grew worse and worse; but when I turned my eyes away from the snarl and kept them fixed on the Lord, He always sooner or later unraveled it and delivered me.

Have you ever watched a farmer plowing a field? If you have, you will have noticed that in order to make straight furrows he is obliged to fix his eyes on a tree, or a post in the fence, or some object at the farther end of the field, and to guide his plow unwaveringly toward that object. If he begins to look back at the furrow behind him in order to see whether he has made a straight furrow, his plow begins to jerk from side to side, and the furrow he is making becomes a zigzag. If we would make straight paths for our feet we must do what the apostle says he did. We must forget the things that are behind, and, reaching forth to those which are before, we must press toward the mark for the prize of the high calling of God in Christ Jesus.

To forget the things that are behind is an essential part of the pressing forward toward the prize of our high calling; and I am convinced this prize can never be reached unless we will consent to this forgetting. When we do consent to it, we come near to putting an end to all our self-examination; for, if we may not look back over our past misdoings, we shall find but little food for self-reflective acts.

We complain of spiritual hunger, and torment ourselves to know why our hunger is not satisfied. The psalmist says: "The eyes of all wait upon thee, and thou givest them their meat in due season." Having our eyes upon ourselves and on our own hunger will never bring a supply of spiritual meat. When a man's larder is empty and he is starving, his eyes are not occupied with looking at the emptiness of his larder, but are turned toward the source from which he hopes or expects to get a supply of food. To examine self is to be like a man who should spend his time in examing his empty larder instead of going to the market for a supply to fill it. No wonder such Christians seem to be starving to death in the midst of all the fullness there is for them in Christ. They never see that fullness, for they never look at it; and again I repeat that the thing we look at is the thing we see.

I feel as if I could not repeat this evident truism too often, for somehow people seem to lay aside their common sense when they come to the subject of religion, and seem to expect to see things upon which they have deliberately kept their backs turned. They cry out, "O Lord, reveal thyself"; but instead of looking at Him they look at themselves, and keep their gaze steadily fixed on their own inward feelings, and then wonder at the "mysterious dealings" of God in hiding His face from their fervent prayers. But how can they see what they do not look at?

It is never God who hides His face from us, but it is always we who hide our face from Him, by "turning to him the back and not the face." The prophet reproaches the children of Israel with this, and adds that they "set up their abominations in the house which is called by God's name." When Christians spend their time examining their own condition, raking up all their sins, and bemoaning their shortcomings, what is this but to set up the "abomination" of their own sinful self upon the chief pedestal in their hearts, and to make it the center of their whole religious life, and of all their care and efforts. They gaze at this great, big, miserable self until it fills their whole horizon, and they "turn their back" on the Lord, until He is lost sight of altogether.

I will venture to say that there are many Christians who, for one look at the Lord, will give a thousand looks at self, and who, for one hour spent in rejoicing in Him, will spend hundreds of hours bemoaning themselves.

We are never anywhere commanded to behold our emotions, nor our experiences, nor even our sins, but we are commanded to turn our backs upon all these, and to behold the Lamb of God who taketh away our sins. One look at Christ is worth more for salvation than a million looks at self. Yet so mistaken are our ideas, we seem unable to avoid thinking that the mortification which results from self-examination must have in it some saving power, because it makes us so miserable. For we have to travel a long way on our heavenly journey before we fully learn that there is no saving power in misery, and that a cheerful, confident faith is the only successful attitude for the aspiring soul.

In Isaiah we see God's people complaining because they fasted, and He did not see; afflicted their souls, and He took no knowledge; and God gave them this significant answer: "Is it such a fast that I have chosen, a day for a man to afflict his soul? Is it to bow down his head as a bulrush, and to spread sackcloth and ashes under him? Wilt thou call this a fast, and an acceptable day to the Lord?" Whoever else is pleased with the miseries of our self-examination, it is very certain that God is not. He does not want us to bow down our heads as a bulrush, any more than He wanted His people of old to do it; and He calls upon us, as He did upon them, to forget our own miserable selves, and to go to work to lessen the miseries of others. "Is not this the fast that I have chosen," He says, "to loose the bands of wickedness, to undo the heavy burdens, and to let the oppressed go free, and that ye break every yoke? Is it not to deal thy bread to the hungry, and that thou bring the poor that are cast out to thy house; when thou seest the naked, that thou cover him?"

This service for others is of infinitely greater value to the Lord than the longest seasons of self-examination and self-abasement. And I am convinced that He has shown us here what is the surest way of deliverance out of the slough of misery into which our habits of self-examination have plunged us. He declares emphatically that if we will only keep the sort of "fast" He approves of, by giving up our own "fast" of afflicting our souls and bowing down our heads as a bulrush, and will instead "draw out our souls to the hungry," and will try to bear the burdens and relieve the miseries of others, then shall our light rise in obscurity, and our darkness be as the noonday; and the Lord shall guide us continually, satisfying our souls in drought, and making fat our bones; we shall be like a watered garden, and like a spring of water whose waters fail not.

All this is exactly what we have been striving for, but our strivings have been in our own way, not in God's. The fast we have chosen has been to afflict our souls, to bow down our heads as bulrushes, and to sit in sackcloth and ashes; and, as a consequence, instead of our bones being made fat, and our souls refreshed like a watered garden, we have found only leanness, and thirst, and misery. Our own fasts, no matter how fervently they may be carried on, nor how many groans and tears may accompany them can never bring us anything else.

Now let us try God's fast. Let us lay aside all care for ourselves, and care instead for our needy brothers and sisters. Let us stop trying to do something for our own poor miserable self-life, and begin to try to do something to help the spiritual lives of others. Let us give up our hopeless efforts to find something in ourselves to delight in, and delight ourselves only in the Lord and in His service. And if we will but do this, all the days of our misery will be ended.

But some may ask whether it is not necessary to examine ourselves in order to find out what is wrong and what needs mending. This would, of course, be necessary if we were our own workmanship, but since we are God's workmanship and not our own, He is the One to examine us, for He is the only One who can tell what is wrong. The man who makes watches is the one to examine a watch when it is out of order, and to set it straight. We have too much good sense to meddle with our watches; why is it that we have not enough good sense to give up meddling with ourselves? Surely we must see that the examining of the Lord is the only kind of examination that is of any use. His examination is like that of a physician who examines in order to cure; while our self-examination is like that of the patient who only becomes more of a hypochondriac the more he examines the symptoms of his disease.

But the question may be asked whether, when there has been actual sin, there ought not to be self-examination and self-reproach at least for a time. This is a fallacy which deceives a great many. It seems too much to believe that we can be forgiven without first going through a season of self-reproach. But what is the Bible teaching? John tells us that if we confess our sins (not bewail them, nor yet try to excuse them), but simply confess them, He is faithful and just to forgive us our sins, and to cleanse us from all unrighteousness. All that God wants is that we should turn to Him at once, acknowledge our sin, and believe in His forgiveness; and every minute that we delay doing this, in order to spend the time in self-examination and self-reproach, is only adding further sin to that which we have already committed. If ever we need to look away from self, and to have our eyes turned to the Lord, it is just when we become conscious of having sinned against Him. The greater the multitude of our enemies, the greater and more immediate our need of God.

All through the Bible we are taught this lesson of death to self and life in Christ alone. "Not I, but Christ," was not intended to be a unique experience of Paul's, but was simply a declaration of what ought to be the experience of every Christian. We sing sometimes, "Thou O Christ, art all I want," but as a fact, we really want a great many other things. We want good feelings, we want fervor and earnestness, we want realizations, we want satisfying experiences; and we continually examine ourselves to try to find out why we do not have these things. We think if we could only discover our points of failure, we should be able to set them straight. But there is no healing or transforming power in gazing at our failures. The only road to Christlikeness is to behold, not our own hatefulness, but His goodness and beauty. We grow like what we look at, and if we spend our lives looking at our hateful selves, we shall become more and more hateful. Do we not find as a fact that self-examination, instead of making us better, always seems to make us worse? Beholding self, we are more and more changed into the image of self. While on the contrary if we spend our time beholding the glory of the Lord, that is, letting our minds dwell upon His goodness and His love, and trying to drink in His spirit, the inevitable result will be that we shall be, slowly perhaps, but surely, changed into the image of the Lord upon whom we are gazing.

Fenelon says that we should never indulge in any self-reflective acts, either of mortification at our failures, or of congratulation at our successes; but that we should continually consign self and all self's doings to oblivion, and should keep our interior eyes upon the Lord only. It is very hard in self-examination not to try to find excuses for our faults; and our self-reflective acts are often in danger of being turned into self-glorying ones. The only way is to ignore self altogether and to forget there is any such being in existence.

No one who does not understand this can possibly appreciate the comfort and relief it is to be done with self and all self-reflective acts. I have known Christian workers whose lives have been one long torment because of these self-reflective acts; and I am convinced that the "Blue Mondays," of which so many clergymen complain, are nothing but the result of an indulgence in self-reflective acts concerning their services in the church the day before.

The only way to treat all forms of self-reflective acts, of whatever kind, is simply to give them up. They always do harm and never good. They are bound to result in one of two things: either they fill us full of self-praise and self-satisfaction, or they plunge us into the depths of discouragement and despair; and whichever it may be, the soul is in this way inevitably shut out from any sight of God and of His salvation.

One of the most effectual ways of conquering the habit is to make a rule that, whenever we are tempted to examine ourselves, we will always at once begin to examine the Lord instead, and will let thoughts of His love and His all-sufficiency sweep out all thoughts of our own unworthiness or our own helplessness.

I have been trying in this book to set the Lord before our eyes in all the beauty of His character and His ways in the hope that the sight will be so ravishing as to take our eyes off everything else. But no revelation of God will be of any use if we will not look at it, but will persist in turning our backs on what has been revealed, and in gazing instead at our own inward experiences. For again I must repeat that we cannot see self and see the Lord at the same time, and that while we are examining self we cannot be looking at Him.

Fenelon says concerning self-examination: "There is something very hidden and very deceptive in the suffering it causes; for while you seem to yourself to be wholly occupied with the glory of God, in your inmost soul it is self alone that occasions all your trouble. You are indeed desirous that God should be glorified, but you wish it should take place by means of your perfection, and you thus cherish the sentiments of self-love. It is simply a refined pretext for dwelling in self ... It is a sort of infidelity to simple faith when we desire to be continually assured that we are doing well. It is, in fact, a desire to know what we are doing, which we shall never know, and of which it is the will of God we should be ignorant. It is trifling by the way, in order to reason about the way. The safest and shortest course is to renounce, forget, and abandon self, and, through faithfulness to God, to think no more of it. This is the whole of religion—to get out of self and self-love in order to get into God."

What we must do, therefore, is to shut the door definitely and resolutely at once and forever upon self, and all of self's experiences, whether they be good or bad; and to say with the psalmist: "I have set the Lord [not self] always before me; because he is at my right hand, I shall not be moved. Therefore my heart is glad, and my glory rejoiceth: my flesh also shall rest in hope."

# Chapter Eleven - Things That Cannot Be Shaken

"And this word, Yet once more, signifies the removing of those things that are shaken, as of things that are made, that those things which cannot be shaken may remain."

After all we have been considering of the unfathomable love and care of God, it might seem to those, who do not understand the deepest ways of love, that no trials or hardness could ever come into the lives of His children. But if we look deeply into the matter, we shall see that often love itself must needs bring the hardness. "Whom the Lord loveth he chasteneth, and scourgeth every son whom he receiveth. If ye endure chastening, God dealeth with you as with sons; for what son is he whom the father chasteneth not? But if ye be without chastisement, whereof all are partakers, then are ye bastards, and not sons."

If love sees those it loves going wrong, it must, because of its very love, do what it can to save them; and the love that fails to do this is only selfishness. Therefore, just because of His unfathomable love, the God of love, when He sees His children resting their souls on things that can be shaken, must necessarily remove those things from their lives in order that they may be driven to rest only on the things that cannot be shaken; and this process of removing is sometimes very hard.

We will all acknowledge, I think, that if our souls are to rest in peace and comfort, it can only be on unshakable foundations. It is no more possible for the soul to be comfortable when it is trying to rest on "things that can be shaken," than it is for the body. No one can rest comfortably in a shaking bed, or sit in comfort on a rickety chair.

Foundations to be reliable must always be unshakable. The house of the foolish man, which is built on the sand, may present a very fine appearance in clear and sunshiny weather; but when storms arise, and the winds blow, and floods come that house will fall, and great will be the fall of it. The wise man's house, on the contrary, which is built on the rock, is able to withstand all the stress of the storm, and remains unshaken through winds and floods, for it is "founded on the rock."

It is very possible in the Christian life to build one's spiritual house on such insecure foundations, that when storms beat upon it, the ruin of that house is great. Many a religious experience that has seemed fair enough when all was going well in life has tottered and fallen when trials have come, because its foundations have been insecure. It is therefore of vital importance to each one of us to see to it that our religious life is built upon "things that cannot be shaken."

Of course the immediate thought that will come to every mind is that it must be "built upon the rock Christ Jesus." This is true; but the great point is what is meant by that expression. It is one of those religious phrases that is often used conventionally with no definite or real meaning attached to it. Conventionally we believe that Christ is the only Rock upon which to build, but practically, though perhaps unconsciously, we believe that in order to have a rock upon which it will be really safe to build, many other things must be added to Christ. We think, for instance, that the right frames and feelings must be added, or the right doctrines or dogmas, or whatever else may seem to each one of us to constitute the necessary degree of security. And if we were only perfectly honest with ourselves, I suspect we should often find that our dependence was almost wholly upon these additions of our own; and that Christ Himself, as our rock of dependence, was of altogether secondary importance.

What we ought to mean when we talk of building upon the Rock Christ Jesus is what I am trying all through this book to make plain, and that is that the Lord is enough for our salvation, just the Lord only without any additions of our own, the Lord Himself, as He is in His own intrinsic character, our Creator and Redeemer, and our all-sufficient portion.

The "foundation of God standeth sure," and it is the only foundation that does. Therefore, we need to be "shaken" from off every other foundation in order that we may be forced to rest on the foundation of God alone. And this explains the necessity for those "shakings" through which so many Christians seem called to pass. The Lord sees that they are building their spiritual houses on flimsy foundations, which will not be able to withstand the "vehement beating" of the storms of life; and not in anger but in tenderest love, He shakes our earth and our heaven until all that "can be shaken" is removed, and only those "things which cannot be shaken" are left behind.

The apostle tells us that the things that are shaken are the "things that are made"; that is, the things that are manufactured by our own efforts, feelings that we get up, doctrines that we elaborate, good works that we perform. It is not that these things are bad things in themselves. It is only when the soul begins to rest on them instead of upon the Lord that He is compelled to "shake" us from off them. And this shaking applies, we are told, "not to the earth only, but also to Heaven." This means, I am sure, that it is possible to have "things that are made" even in religious matters.

How much of the so-called religiousness of many Christians consists of these "things that are made," I cannot say; but I sometimes think the great overturnings and tossings in matters of faith, which so distress Christians in these times, may be only the necessary shaking of the "things that are made," in order that only that which "cannot be shaken" may remain.

There are times, it may be, in our religious lives, when our experience seems to us as settled and immovable as the roots of the everlasting mountains. But there comes an upheaval, and all our foundations are shaken and thrown down, and we are ready to despair and to question whether we can be Christians at all. Sometimes it is an upheaval in our outward circumstances, and sometimes it is in our inward experience. If people have rested on their good words and their faithful service, the Lord is often obliged to take away all power for work or else all opportunity in order that the soul may be driven from its false resting place and forced to rest in the Lord alone. Sometimes the dependence is upon good feelings or pious emotions, and the soul has to be deprived of these before it can learn to depend only upon God. Sometimes it is upon "sound doctrine" that the dependence is placed, and the man feels himself to be occupying an invulnerable position, because his views are so correct, and his doctrines are so orthodox; and then the Lord is obliged to shake his doctrines, and to plunge him, it may be, into confusion and darkness as to his views.

It was at just such a moment as this that my own soul caught its first real sight of God; and what had seemed certain spiritual ruin and defeat was turned into the most triumphant victory.

Or it may be that the upheaval comes in our outward circumstances. Everything has seemed so firmly established in prosperity that no dream of disaster disturbs us. Our reputation is assured, our work has prospered, our efforts have all been successful beyond our hopes, and our soul is at ease; and the need for God is in danger of becoming far off and vague. And then the Lord is obliged to put an end to it all, and our prosperity crumbles around us like a house built on sands, and we are tempted to think He is angry with us. But in very truth it is not anger, but tenderest love. His very love it is that compels Him to take away the outward prosperity that is keeping our souls from entering into the interior spiritual kingdom for which we long. When the fig tree ceases to blossom, and there is not fruit in the vines; when the labor of the olive shall fail, and the fields shall yield no meat; when the flock shall be cut off from the fold, and there shall be no herd in the stalls, then, and often not until then, will our souls learn to rejoice in the Lord only, and to joy in the God of our salvation.

Paul declared that he counted all things but loss that he might win Christ; and when we learn to say the same, the peace and joy that the Gospel promises become our permanent possession.

"What iniquity," asks the Lord of the children of Israel, "have your fathers found in me that they are gone far from me and have walked after vanity? For my people have committed two evils; they have forsaken me, the fountain of living waters, and hewed them out cisterns, broken cisterns that can hold no water." Like the Israelites, we too forsake the fountain of living waters, and try to hew out for ourselves cisterns of our own devising. We seek to slake our thirst with our own experiences or our own activities, and then wonder that we still thirst. And it is to save us from perishing for want of water that the Lord finds it necessary to destroy our broken cisterns; since only so can we be forced to drink from the fountain of living waters.

We are told that if we "trust in vanity," vanity shall be our recompense; and many a time have we found this to be true. Have you ever crossed a dangerous swamp abounding in quicksands, where every step was a risk, and where firm-looking hillocks continually deceived you into a false dependence, causing you to sink in the mire and water concealed beneath their deceptive appearances? If you have, you will be able to understand what it means to "trust in vanity," and you will appreciate the blessedness of any dispensation that shall discover to you the rottenness of your false dependencies, and shall drive you to trust in that which is safe and permanent. When our feet are walking on "miry clay," we can have nothing but welcome for the divine Guide who shall bring us out from the clay, and shall "set our feet upon a rock," and "establish our goings," even though the ways in which He calls us to walk may seem narrow and hard.

The prophet Jeremiah, when lamenting the sins of his people, says: "We have made lies our refuge, and under falsehoods have we hid ourselves," and he adds that the Lord had declared He would sweep away the refuge of lies, and would cause the waters to overflow the hiding place. It might look, as far as the outward seeming goes, as though it was God's wrath that did this, and many a frightened Christian thinks it is; but His wrath is only against the refuges of lies, not against us, and love could do no less than destroy these refuges in order that we may be delivered.

A dear old friend of mine, who was very much interested in my spiritual welfare, gave me a little book called, The Seventeen False Rests of the Soul, evidently feeling that I was in danger of settling down upon one or another of these false rests. The book set forth in quaint old language the idea that the soul was continually tempted to sit down upon some falsity, as though it were a final resting place, and that God was continually obliged to "unbottom" all such false resting places, as though one should unbottom a chair and let the sitter fall through. All these seventeen false rests were described, and it was shown how the soul, being "unbottomed" off each one successively, settled down at last upon the only true rest in God. This "unbottoming" is only another word for the "shakings" and "emptyings" of which I have been writing. It is always a painful process, and often a most discouraging one. Everything seems unstable, and rest seems utterly unattainable. No sooner do we find an experience or a doctrine in which we think we may surely rest, than a great "shaking" comes, and we are forced out again. And this process must continue until all that can be shaken is removed, and only "those things which cannot be shaken" remain.

Often the answer to our most fervent prayers for deliverance comes in such a form that it seems as if the "very foundations of the hills moved and were shaken"; and we do not always see at first that it is by means of this very shaking that the deliverance for which we have prayed is to be accomplished, and we are to be brought forth into the "large place" for which we long.

The old mystics used to teach what they called "detachment"; meaning the cutting loose of the soul from all that could hold it back from God. This need for "detachment" is the secret of many of our "shakings." We cannot follow the Lord fully so long as we are tied fast to anything else, any more than a boat can sail out into the boundless ocean so long as it is tied fast to the shore.

If we could reach the "city which hath sure and steadfast foundations," we must go out like Abraham from all other cities, and must be detached from every earthly tie. Everything in Abraham's life that could be shaken was shaken. He was, as it were, emptied from vessel to vessel, here today and gone tomorrow; all his resting places were disturbed, and no settlement or comfort anywhere. We, like Abraham, are looking for a city which hath foundations, whose builder and maker is God, and therefore we too shall need to be emptied from vessel to vessel. But we do not realize this, and when the overturnings and shakings come, we are in despair and think we shall never reach the city that hath foundations at all. But it is these very shakings that make it possible for us to reach it. The psalmist had learned this, and after all the shakings and emptying of his eventful life, he cried: "My soul, wait thou only upon God; for my expectation is from him. He only is my rock and my salvation: he is my defense; I shall not be moved. In God is my salvation and my glory: the rock of my strength and my refuge is in God."

At last God was everything to him; and then he found that God was enough.

And it is the same with us. When everything in our lives and experience is shaken that can be shaken, and only that which cannot be shaken remains, we are brought to see that God only is our rock and our foundation, and we learn to have our expectation from Him alone.

"Therefore will not we fear though the earth be removed, and though the mountains be carried into the midst of the sea; though the waters thereof roar and be troubled, though the mountains shake with the swelling thereof ... God is in the midst of her, she shall not be moved. God shall help her, and that right early." "Shall not be moved"—what an inspiring declaration! Can it be possible that we, who are so easily moved by the things of earth, can arrive at a place where nothing can upset our temper or disturb our calm? Yes, it is possible; and the apostle Paul knew it. When he was on his way to Jerusalem, where he foresaw that "bonds and afflictions" awaited him, he could say triumphantly, "But none of these things move me." Everything in Paul's life and experience that could be shaken had been shaken, and he no longer counted his life, or any of life's possessions, dear unto him. And we, if we will but let God have His way with us, may come to the same place so that neither the fret and fear of the little things of life, nor its great and heavy trials, can have power to move us from the peace that passeth all understanding, which is declared to be the portion of those who have learned to rest only on God.

In that wonderful Revelation made to John in the "isle that is called Patmos," where the Spirit tells to the churches what awaits those who overcome, we have a statement that expresses in striking terms just what I mean. "Him that overcometh will I make a pillar in the temple of my God; and he shall go no more out." To be as immovable as a pillar in the house of our God is an end for which one would gladly endure all the "shakings" and "unbottomings" that may be necessary to bring us there!

"Wherefore we receiving a kingdom that cannot be moved, let us have grace whereby we may serve God acceptably with reverence and godly fear; for our God is a consuming fire." A great many people are afraid of the consuming fire of God, but that is only because they do not understand what it is. It is the fire of God's love, that must in the very nature of things consume everything that can harm His people; and if our hearts are set on being what the love of God would have us be, His fire is something we shall not be afraid of, but shall warmly welcome.

*Implacable is love.*
*Foes may be bought or teased*
*From their malign intent;*
*But he goes unappeased,*
*Who is on kindness bent.*

Let us thank God, then, that He is "on kindness bent" toward us, and that the consuming fire of His love will not cease to burn until it has refined us as silver is refined. For the promise is that He shall sit as a refiner and purifier of silver, and He shall purge us as gold and silver are purged in order that we may offer unto Him an offering in righteousness; and He gives us this inspiring assurance, that if we will but submit to this purifying process, we shall become "pleasant unto the Lord," and all nations shall call us blessed, "for ye shall be a delightsome land, saith the Lord of Hosts."

To be "pleasant" and delightsome" to the Lord may seem to us impossible, when we look at our shortcomings and our unworthiness. But when we think of this lovely, consuming fire of God's love, we can be of good heart and take courage, for He will not fail nor be discouraged until all our dross and reprobate silver is burned up, and we ourselves come forth in His likeness and are conformed to His image.

Our souls long for the "kingdom which cannot be moved," and He "who is on kindness bent," will, if we will let Him, shake everything in our lives that can be shaken, and will unbottom us off every false rest, until only that which cannot be shaken shall remain.

One of the most impressive sermons I ever heard was preached by a sweet-faced old Quaker lady, who rose in the stillness and said, "Yesterday Sister Tabitha broke all to pieces my best china teapot, but the Lord, whom I trust, kept my soul in perfect peace, and enabled me not to utter a single word of reproach." That was all; the sermon ended; but into every heart there entered a sense of what it would mean to be kept in the immovable kingdom of the love of God.

And this kingdom may be our home, if we will but submit to the shakings of God, and will learn to rest only and always on Him.

May He hasten the day for each one of us!

# Chapter Twelve - A Word To The Wavering Ones

"But let him ask in faith, nothing wavering. For he that wavereth is like a wave of the sea driven with the wind and tossed. For let not that man think that he shall receive anything of the Lord."

It would be difficult to find any one thing that produces more discomfort in the religious life than does a wavering faith. The figure given us by the apostle James exactly describes it—"a wave of the sea driven by the wind and tossed." And just as it is impossible for a traveler to reach his destination by advancing one day, and retracing his steps the next, so is it equally impossible for the wavering soul, while it wavers, to reach any place of settled peace.

In our last chapter we considered the shakings of God; and it might be thought that our waverings would be akin to His shakings. But God's shakings are caused by His love, and are for our blessing, and always lead to rest and peace; while our waverings are caused by our want of faith, and always lead to discomfort and turmoil.

A wavering Christian is a Christian who trusts in the love of God one day and doubts it the next, and who is alternately happy or miserable accordingly. He mounts to the hilltop of joy at one time, only to descend at another time into the valley of despair. He is driven to and fro by every wind of doctrine, is always striving and never attaining, and is a prey to each changing influence, caused by his state of health, or by the influences around him, or even by the state of the weather.

You would suppose that even the most ignorant child of God would know without telling that this sort of experience is all wrong, and that to waver in one's faith after such a fashion is one of the things most dishonoring to the Lord, whose truth and faithfulness it so impugns. But as a fact, there are many Christians whose eyes are so blinded in the matter, that they actually think this tendency to waver is a tribute to the humility of their spirits, and who exalt every fresh attack of doubt into a secret and most pious virtue. A wavering Christian will say complacently, "Oh, but I know myself to be so unworthy, that I am sure it is right for me to doubt," and they will imply by their tone of superiority, that their hearer, if truly humble, would doubt also.

In fact, I knew one really devoted Christian, whose religious life was one long torment of doubt, who said to me once in solemn earnestness, after I had been urging him to have more faith, "My dear friend, if once I should be so presumptuous as to feel sure that God loved me, I should be certain I was on the direct road to hell." He thought, no doubt, that such an assurance could only arise from a feeling that he was good enough to be worthy of God's love, and that to feel this would be presumption. And in this he would have been right, for to think ourselves good enough to be worthy of God's love would be presumption indeed. But the ground for our assurance is not to come from our own goodness, but from the goodness of God; and while we never can be and never ought to be satisfied with the first, there cannot possibly be any question to one who believes the Bible as to the all-sufficiency of the last.

To see the absurdity, not to call it by any harsher name, of the position of doubt taken up by this dear Christian, it is only necessary to consider how it would work with any of our human relations in life. Try to imagine what it would be in the marriage relation, or in the relation of children to a parent, both of which relations are used by the Lord as figures of our relation to Himself. Suppose either wife or husband should have a wavering experience of confidence in the other, one day trusting, and the next day doubting; would this be considered a sign of true humility on the doubter's part, and therefore a thing to be cherished as a virtue? Or, similarly, if children should waver in their confidence toward their earthly parents, as Christians seem to feel at liberty to do with their heavenly Parent, what name could be found severe enough by which to call such unofficial conduct? Of course in earthly relations such wavering might come from the fact that one of the parties concerned was unworthy of confidence, and in this case it could be excused. But in the case of God there could not possibly be any such excuse; although the wavering faith of some of His children may, I am afraid, sometimes lead outsiders to conclude that He cannot be worthy of much confidence, or their faith would be more steadfast.

We would shrink in horror from being the cause of any such imputation on the character of God; but I think, if we are honest with ourselves, we will be forced to acknowledge that our wavering faith is calculated to convey just such an impression; and that it really is, therefore, in its essence disloyalty to a trustworthy God, and should be mourned over as a grievous sin. The truth is, although we may not know it, our wavering comes, not from humility, but from a subtle and often unconscious form of pride. True humility accepts the love that is bestowed upon it, and the gifts of that love, with a meek and happy thankfulness, while pride shrinks from accepting gifts and kindnesses, and is afraid to believe in the disinterested goodness of the one who bestows them. Were we truly humble, we would accept God's love with thankful meekness, and, while acknowledging our own unworthiness, would only think of it as enhancing His grace and goodness in choosing us as the recipients of such blessings.

A wavering faith is not only disloyal to God, but it is a source of untold misery to ourselves, and cannot in any way advance our spiritual interests, but must always under all circumstances hinder and upset them. The apostle tells us that we are made partakers of Christ if we "hold the beginning of our confidence steadfast unto the end." To be steadfast is the exact contrary of wavering, and to expect the results of steadfastness as the outcome of wavering is as foolish as it would be to expect to reach the top of a mountain by alternately climbing two steps and sliding back three. And yet many people expect this very thing. They make a "beginning of confidence," and for a little time, while the freshness of it lasts, are full of joy and triumph. Then trials come, and temptations; and doubts begin to intrude; and instead of treating these doubts as enemies to be resisted and driven away, they receive them as friends, and give them entertainment; and sooner or later they begin to waver in their faith and in their allegiance, and from that moment all settled peace is gone. When skies are bright and all goes well with them, their faith revives, and they are happy; but when skies are dark and things go wrong doubts triumph, and they waver again.

I was having a conversation with a very eminent clergyman on the possibility of a religious life of abiding peace and rest, and he told me frankly that he did not believe it was possible, and that he thought most Christian experience was like his own. "Now I," he said, "when I want to write my sermons, I get up on the mountaintop by prayer and by climbing. I put my foot first on one promise and then on another, and so, by hard climbing and much praying, I reach the summit, and can begin my sermon. All goes swimmingly for a little while, and then suddenly an interruption comes, some trouble with my children, or some domestic upset in the house, or some quarrel with a neighbor, and down I tumble from the mountaintop, and can only get back again by another wearisome climb. "Sometimes," he said, "I stay on the summit for two or three days, and once in a great while, even for two or three weeks. But as to there being any possibility of being seated in heavenly places in Christ, and abiding there continually, I cannot believe it."

I am sure this will describe the experience of many of God's children, who are hungering and thirsting for the peace and rest Christ has promised them, but who seem unable to attain to it for more than a few moments at a time. They may get now and then a faint glimmer of faith, and peace seems to be coming, and then all the old doubts spring up again with tenfold power. "Look at your heart," they say; "see how cold it is, how indifferent. How can you for a moment believe that God can love such a poor, unworthy creature as you are?" And it all sounds so reasonable that they are plunged into darkness again.

The whole trouble arises from a want of faith. It seems commonplace to say it, for I have to say it so often, but in the spiritual life it is to us always, always, ALWAYS according to our faith. This is a spiritual law that can neither be neglected nor evaded. It is not an arbitrary law which we might hope could be repealed in our own especial case, but it is inherent in the very nature of things, and is therefore unalterable. And equally inherent in the nature of things is its converse, that if it is to be to us according to our faith, so will it also be to us according to our doubts.

The whole root and cause then of our wavering experience is not, as we may have thought, our sins, but is simply and only our doubts. Doubts create an impassable gulf between our souls and the Lord, just as inevitably as they do between us and our earthly friends; and no amount of fervor or earnestness can bridge this gulf in one case any more than in the other. "Let not that man that wavereth think that he shall receive anything of the Lord." This is not because God is angry, and visits His displeasure in this way on the man who doubts, but it is because of that inherent nature of things that makes it impossible for doubt and confidence to exist together, whether in earthly relations or heavenly, and which neither God nor man can alter. "To whom sware he that they should not enter into his rest but to them that believed not. So we see they could not enter in because of unbelief." It was not that God would not allow them to enter in as a punishment for their unbelief, but they simply could not. It was an impossibility. Faith is the only door into the kingdom of Heaven, and there is no other. If we will not go in by that door, we cannot get in at all, for there is no other way.

God's salvation is not a purchase to be made, nor wages to be earned, nor a summit to be climbed, nor a task to be accomplished; but it is simply and only a gift to be accepted, and can only be accepted by faith. Faith is a necessary element in the acceptance of any gift, whether earthly or heavenly. My friends may put their gifts upon my table, or even place them in my lap, but unless I believe in their friendliness and honesty of purpose enough to accept these gifts, they can never become really mine.

It is plain, therefore, that the Bible is simply announcing, as it always does, the nature of things, when it declares that "according to your faith" it shall be unto you. And the sooner we settle down to this the better. All our wavering comes from the fact that we do not believe in this law. We acknowledge, of course, that it is in the Bible, but we think it cannot really mean what it says, and that there must be some additions made to it; for instance, as "according to our fervency it shall be unto us," or "according to our importunity," or "according to our worthiness." And, if the whole truth were told, we are inclined to think that these additions of ours are, if anything, by far the most important part of the whole matter. As a consequence of this, our attention is mostly directed to getting these matters settled, and we watch our own frames and feelings, and search into our own worthiness or unworthiness with so much assiduity that we overlook almost altogether the one fundamental principle of faith, without which nothing whatever can be done. Moreover, as our disposition and feelings are the most variable things in the universe, and our sense of worthiness or unworthiness changes with our changing feelings, our experience cannot but waver; and the possibility of a steadfast faith recedes farther and farther into the background. We in short make the faithfulness of God, and the truth of His Word, depend upon the state of our feelings.

I am very certain that if any of our friends should treat us in this doubting fashion, we would be wounded and indignant beyond measure; and no feeling of unworthiness on their part could excuse them in our eyes for such a wavering of their confidence in us. In fact, we would far rather our friends should even sin against us than doubt us. No form of sinfulness ever hindered the Lord Jesus while on earth from doing His mighty works. The only thing that hindered Him was unbelief. In His own town, and among His own neighbors and friends, where naturally He would have liked to have performed some of His miracles, we are told that, "He did not many mighty works there because of their unbelief." It was not that He would not, but simply that He could not. And He cannot in our case, any more than in theirs.

But I am afraid some of you may think I am making a mistake, and that, in spite of what God has said, the man whose faith wavers can after all, if he is only fervent and earnest enough, receive something from the Lord. That means that you do not believe that God understands the laws of His kingdom as well as you yourself do, and that it is safer to follow your own ideas rather than His Word. And yet you must know that hitherto your doubts have brought you nothing but darkness and misery. Recall the days, and weeks, and even perhaps months and years of a halting, stumbling, uncomfortable, religious life, and ask yourself honestly whereto the cause of it all has not been your wavering faith. If you believe one day that God loves you and is favorable to you, and the next day doubt His love, and fear He is angry with you, does it not stand to reason that you must waver in your experience from joy to misery; and that only a steadfast faith in His love and care could give you an unwavering experience?

The one question, therefore, for all whose faith wavers is how to put an end at once and forever to their wavering. And here I am thankful to say that I know of a perfect remedy The only thing you have to do is to give it up. Your wavering is caused by your doubting, and by nothing else. Give up your doubting, and your wavering will stop. Keep on with your doubting, and your wavering will continue. The whole matter is as simple as daylight; and the choice is in your own hands.

Perhaps you may think this is an extreme statement, for it has probably never entered your heads that you could give up doubting altogether. But I assert that you can. You can simply refuse to doubt. You can shut the door against every suggestion of doubt that comes, and can by faith declare exactly the opposite. Your doubt says, "God does not forgive my sins." Your faith must say, "He does forgive me; He says He does, and I choose to believe Him. I am His forgiven child." And you must assert this steadfastly, until all your doubts vanish. You have no more right to say that you are of such a doubting nature that you cannot help doubting, than to say you are of <unclear>such a easily</unclear> controlled as the other. You must give up your doubting just as you would give up your thieving. You must treat the temptation to doubt exactly as a drunkard must treat the temptation to drink; you must take a pledge against it.

The process I believe to be the most effectual is to lay our doubts, just as we lay our other sins, upon God's altar, and make a total surrender of them. We must give up all liberty to doubt, and must consecrate our power of believing to Him, and must trust Him to keep us trusting. We must make our faith in His Word as inevitable and necessary a thing as is our obedience to His will. We must be as loyal to our heavenly Friend as we are to our earthly friends, and must refuse to recognize the possibility of such thing as any questioning or doubting of His love or His faithfulness, or of any wavering in our absolute faith in His Word.

Of course temptations to waver will come, and it will sometimes look to us impossible that the Lord can love such disagreeable, unworthy beings as we feel ourselves to be. But we must turn as deaf an ear to these insinuations against the love of God as we would to any insinuations against the love of our dearest friend. The fight to do this may sometimes be very severe, and may even at times seem almost unendurable. But our unchanging declaration must continually be, "though he slay me, yet will I trust in him." Our steadfast faith will unfailingly bring us, sooner or later, a glorious victory.

Probably it will often seem to us as if it would be a righteous thing, in view of our many shortcomings, and only what a truly humble soul would do, to waver in our faith and to question whether the salvation of the Lord Jesus can be meant for us. But if we at all understand what the salvation of the Lord Jesus Christ is, we cannot fail to recognize that all this is only temptation; and that what we must do is to lift up the shield of faith persistently against it; for the shield of faith always does and always will quench every fiery dart of the enemy.

The Spirit of God never under any circumstance could suggest a doubt of the love of God. Wherever doubts come from, one thing is certain, they do not come from Heaven. All doubts are from an evil source, and they must always be treated as the suggestions of an enemy. We cannot, it is true, prevent the suggestions of doubt making themselves heard in our hearts, any more than we can prevent our ears from hearing the oaths of wicked men in the streets. But just as we can refuse to approve of or join in the oaths of these men, so can we refuse to pay any attention to these suggestions of doubt. The cases are exactly similar. But while in the case of the oaths, we know without any question that it would be wicked to join in with them, in the case of the doubts we have a lurking feeling that, after all, doubts may have something pious in them, and ought to be encouraged. But I believe one is as displeasing to God as the other.

Again I would repeat that the only way to treat the doubts that make you waver is to give them up. An absolute surrender is the only remedy. It is like the drunkard with his drink, half measures are of no manner of use. Total abstinence is the only hope.

The most practical way of doing this is not only to make the interior surrender, but to meet, as I have said, each doubt with a flat denial; and to carry the war into the enemy's country, as it were, by an emphatic assertion of faith in direct opposition to the doubt. For instance, if the doubt arises as to whether God can love anyone so sinful and unfaithful as you feel yourself to be, you must at once assert in definite words in your own heart, and if possible aloud to someone, that God does love you; that He says He does, and that His Word is a million times more trustworthy than any of your feelings, no matter how well founded they may seem to you to be. If you cannot find anyone to whom to say this, then write it in a letter, or else say it aloud to yourself and to God. Be very definite about it.

If in anything you have had a "beginning of confidence," if you have ever laid hold of any promise or declaration of the Lord's, hold on steadfastly to that promise or declaration without wavering, let come what may. There can be no middle ground. If it was true once, it is true still, for God is unchangeable. The only thing that can deprive you of it is your unbelief. While you believe, you have it. "Whatsoever things ye desire when ye pray, believe that ye receive them and ye shall have them."

Let nothing shake your faith. Should even sin unhappily overtake you, you must not let it make you doubt. At once, on the discovery of any sin, take I John 1:9 and act on it. "If we confess our sins, he is faithful and just to forgive us our sins, and to cleanse us from all unrighteousness." Confess your sin, therefore, immediately upon the discovery of it, and believe at once that God does forgive it, as He declares, and does again cleanse you from all unrighteousness. No sin, however grievous, can separate us from God for one moment, after it has been treated in this fashion. To allow sin to cause your faith to waver is only to add a new sin to the one already committed. Return at once to God in the way the Bible teaches, and let your faith hold steadfastly to His Word. Believe it, not because you feel it, or see it, but because He says it. Believe it, even when it seems to you that you are believing a lie. Believe it actively and steadfastly, through dark and through light, through ups and through downs, through times of comfort and through times of despair, and I can promise you, without a fear, that your wavering experience will be ended.

"Therefore, beloved brethren, be ye steadfast, immovable, always abounding in the work of the Lord, forasmuch as ye know that your labor is not in vain in the Lord." To be "immovable" in one's religious life is the exact opposite of wavering. In the Forty-sixth Psalm we can see what it is. The earth may be removed, and the mountains may be carried into the midst of the sea, our whole universe may seem to be in ruins, but while we trust in the Lord we "shall not be moved."

The man who wavers in his faith is upset by the smallest trifles; the man who is steadfast in his faith can look on calmly at the ruin of all his universe.

To be thus immovable in one's religious life is a boon most ardently to be desired, and it may be ours if we will only hold the beginning of our confidence steadfast to the end.

*Faith is sweetest of worships to him who so loves*
*His unbearable splendors in darkness to hide;*
*And to trust in Thy Word, dearest Lord, is true love,*
*For those prayers are most granted which seem most denied.*
*And faith throws her arms around all Thou hast told her,*
*And able to hold as much more, can but grieve;*
*She could hold Thy grand self, Lord! if Thou wouldst reveal it.*
*And love makes her long to have more to believe.*

# Chapter Thirteen - Discouragement

"The soul of the people was much discouraged because of the way."

The church of Christ abounds with people who are "discouraged because of the way." Either inwardly or outwardly, and oftentimes both, things look all wrong, and there seems no hope of escape. Their souls faint in them, and their religious lives are full of discomfort and misery. There is nothing that so paralyzes effort as discouragement, and nothing that more continually and successfully invites defeat. The secret of failure or success in any matter lies far more in the soul's interior attitude than in any other cause or causes. It is a law of our being, which is only now beginning to be discovered, that the inward man counts for far more in every conflict than anything the outward man do or may possess.

And nowhere is this truer than in the spiritual life. Again I must repeat what I find it necessary to say so continually, that the Bible declares from beginning to end that faith is the law of the spiritual life, and that according to our faith it always shall be and always will be unto us. Then, since faith and discouragement cannot, in the very nature of things, exist together, it is perfectly manifest that discouragement must be an absolute barrier to faith. And that where discouragement rules, the converse to the law of faith must rule also, and it shall be to us, not according to our faith, but according to our discouragement.

In fact, just as courage is faith in good, so discouragement is faith in evil; and, while courage opens the door to good, discouragement opens it to evil.

An allegory that I heard very early in my Christian life has always remained in my memory as one of those warnings to motorists that we often see at the top of hills on country roads, "This hill is dangerous"; and it has many a time warned me away from the dangerous descent of discouragement.

The allegory declared that once upon a time Satan, who desired to entrap a devoted Christian worker, allied a council of his helpers to decide on the best way of doing it, and to ask for volunteers. After the case had been explained, an imp offered himself to do the work.

"How will you do it?" asked Satan.

"Oh," replied the imp, "I will paint to him the delights and pleasures of a life of sin in such glowing colors that he will be eager to enter upon it."

"That will not do," said Satan, shaking his head. "The man has tried sin, and he knows better. He knows it leads to misery and ruin, and he will not listen to you."

Then another imp offered himself, and again Satan asked, "What will you do to win the man over?"

"I will picture to him the trials and the self-denials of a righteous life, and will make him eager to escape from them."

"Ah, that will not do either," said Satan, "for he has tried righteousness, and he knows that its paths are paths of peace and happiness."

Then a third imp started up and declared that he was sure he could bring the man over.

"Why, what will you do," asked Satan, "that you are so sure?"

"I will discourage his soul," replied the imp triumphantly.

"That will do, that will do," exclaimed Satan, "you will be successful. Go and bring back your victim."

An old Quaker has this saying, "All discouragement is from the Devil"; and I believe he stated a far deeper and more universal truth than we have yet fully understood. Discouragement cannot have its source in God. The religion of the Lord Jesus Christ is a religion of faith, of good cheer, of courage, of hope that maketh not ashamed. "Be discouraged," says our lower nature, "for the world is a place of temptation and sin." "Be of good cheer," says Christ, "for I have overcome the world." There cannot possibly be any room for discouragement in a world which Christ has overcome.

We must settle it then, once for all, that discouragement comes from an evil source, only and always. I know this is not the general idea, at least in the spiritual region of things. In temporal things, perhaps, we have more or less learned that discouragement is foolish, and even wrong; but, when it comes to spiritual things, we are apt to reverse the order, and make that commendable in one case, which is reprehensible in the other; and we even succeed in persuading ourselves that to be discouraged is a very pious state of mind, and an evidence of true humility.

The causes for our discouragement seem so legitimate, that to be discouraged seems to our short-sightedness the only right and proper state of mind to cultivate. The first and perhaps the most common of these causes is the fact of our own incapacity. It is right for us to be cast down, we think, because we know ourselves to be such poor, miserable, good-for-nothing creatures. It would be presumption, in the face of such incapacity, to be anything but discouraged.

Moses is an illustration of this. The Lord had called him to lead the children of Israel out of the land of Egypt; and Moses, looking at this own natural infirmities and weaknesses, was discouraged, and tried to excuse himself: "I am not eloquent, but I am slow of speech and of a slow tongue. They will not believe me nor hearken unto my voice." Naturally, one would think that Moses had plenty of cause for discouragement, and for discouragement very similar to that which is likely to assail us, when, because of our distrust in our own eloquence, or our own power to convince those to whom we are to be sent, we shrink from the work to which the Lord may be calling us. But notice how the Lord answered Moses, for in the same way I am convinced does He answer us. He did not do, what no doubt Moses would have liked best, try to convince him that he really was eloquent, or that his tongue was not slow of speech. He passed all this by as being of no account whatever, and simply called attention to the fact that, since He had made man's mouth and would Himself be with the mouth He had made, there could not possibly be any cause for discouragement, even if Moses did have all the infirmities of speech of which he had complained. "And the Lord said unto him, Who hath made man's mouth? or who maketh the dumb, or deaf, or the seeing, or the blind? Have not I, the Lord? Now therefore go, and I will be with thy mouth, and teach thee what thou shalt say."

When the word of the Lord came to Jeremiah telling him that He had organized him to be a prophet to the nations, Jeremiah felt himself to be entirely unequal to such a work, and said: "Ah, Lord God, behold, I cannot speak, for I am a child." But the Lord answered: "Say not, I am a child; for thou shalt go to all that I shall send thee, and whatever I say to thee, thou shalt speak. Be not afraid of their faces, for I am with thee to deliver thee, saith the Lord."

Gideon is another illustration. The Lord had called him to undertake the deliverance of His people from the oppression of the Midianites, and had said to him: "Go in this thy might, and thou shalt save Israel from the hands of the Midianites: have I not sent thee?" This ought to have been enough for Gideon, but he was a poor unknown man, of no family or position, and no apparent fitness for such a great mission; and, looking at himself and his own deficiencies, he naturally became discouraged, and said: "Wherewith shall I save Israel? Behold, my family is poor in Manasseh, and I am the least in my father's house." Other men, he felt, who had power and influence, might perhaps accomplish this great work, but not one so poor and insignificant as himself. How familiar this sort of talk must sound to the victims of discouragement among my readers, and how sensible and reasonable it seems! But what did the Lord think of it? "And the Lord said unto him, Surely I will be with thee, and thou shalt smite the Midianites as one man"—simply and only the promise, "Surely I will be with thee." Not one word of encouragement did He give Gideon, nor does He give us as to our own capacities or fitness for the work required, but merely the bare statement of the fact of being sufficient for all possible needs, "I will be with thee." To all words of discouragement in the Bible this is the invariable answer, "I will be with thee"; and it is an answer that precludes all possibility of argument or of any further discouragement. I thy Creator and thy Redeemer, I thy strength and thy wisdom, I thy omnipresent and omniscient God, I will be with thee, and will protect thee through everything; no enemy shall hurt thee, no strife of tongues shall disturb thee; My presence shall be thy safety and thy sure defense.

One would think that in the face of such assertions as these not even the most fainthearted among us could find any loophole for discouragement. But discouragement comes in many subtle forms, and our spiritual enemies attack us in many disguises. Our own especial make-up or temperament is one of the most common and insidious of our enemies. Other people, who are made differently, can be cheerful and courageous, we think, but it is right that we should be discouraged when we see the sort of people we are, how foolish, how helpless, how unfit to grapple with any enemies! And there would indeed be ample cause for discouragement if we were to be called upon to fight our battles ourselves. We would be right in thinking we could not do it. But if the Lord is to fight them for us, it puts an entirely different complexion on the matter, and our want of ability to fight becomes an advantage instead of a disadvantage. We can only be strong in Him when we are weak in ourselves, and our weakness, therefore, is in reality our greatest strength.

The children of Israel can give us a warning lesson here. After the Lord had delivered them out of Egypt, and had brought them to the borders of the promised land, Moses urged them to go up and possess it. "Behold," he said, "the Lord thy God hath set the land before thee; go up and possess it, as the Lord God of thy fathers hath said unto thee; fear not, neither be discouraged." But the circumstances were so discouraging, and they felt themselves to be so helpless, that they could not believe God would really do all He had said; and they murmured in their tents, and declared that it must be because the Lord hated them that He had brought them out of Egypt in order to deliver them into the hands of their enemies. "And they said, Whither shall we go up? Our brethren have discouraged our heart, saying, The people is greater and taller than we; the cities are great and walled up to heaven; and moreover we have seen the sons of the Anakims there."

When we read the report of the spies we cannot be surprised at their discouragement; and we can even believe they would have felt that courage under such circumstances would be only foolhardiness. "The land through which we have gone to search it," the spies declared, "is a land that eateth up the inhabitants thereof: and all the men that we saw in it are men of a great stature. And there we saw the giants, the sons of Anak, which come of the giants: and we were in our own sight as grasshoppers, and so we were in their sight." Nothing could have seemed humbler than for them to look upon themselves as poor, good-for-nothing grasshoppers; and true humility would have seemed to teach that it would be the height of presumption for grasshoppers to try to conquer giants. We also often feel ourselves to be but grasshoppers in the face of the giants of temptation and trouble that assail us, and we think ourselves justified in being discouraged. But the question is not, whether we are grasshoppers, but whether God is; for it is not we who have to fight these giants, but God.

In vain, Moses reminded the Israelites of this. In vain he assured them that they had no need to be afraid of even the sons of the Anakims, for the Lord their God would fight for them. He even reminded them of past deliverances, and asked them if they did not remember how that "in the wilderness the Lord thy God bear thee as a man doth bear his son in all the way that ye went"; but they were still too discouraged to believe. And the result was that not one of that "evil generation" was allowed to see the Promised Land, except only Caleb and Joshua, who had steadfastly believed that God could and would lead them in.

Such are the fruits of giving way to discouragement, and such is the reward of a steadfast faith.

The apostle in commenting on this story in Hebrews says: "And to whom sware he that they should not enter into his rest, but to them that believed not? So we see that they could not enter in because of unbelief."

Is there no parallel in all this to our case? Do we not look at our weakness instead of looking at the Lord's strength; and have we not sometimes become so discouraged as to sink into such "anguish of spirit," that we cannot even hearken to the Lord's own declarations that He will fight for us and will give us the victory? Our souls long to enter into the rest the Lord has promised; but giants and cities great and walled up to Heaven seem to stand in our pathway, and we are afraid to believe. So we too, like the Israelites, cannot enter in because of unbelief.

How different it would be if we only had faith enough to say with the psalmist: "Though an host should encamp against me, my heart shall not fear; though war should rise against me, in this will I be confident...For in the time of trouble he shall hide me in his pavilion: in the secret of his tabernacle he shall hide me. He shall set me up upon a rock." How joyfully and triumphantly would we be able to enter into rest, if this were our language!

Another very subtle cause for discouragement is to be found in what is called the fear of man. There seems to exist in this world a company of beings called "they" who lord it over life with an iron hand of control. What will "they" say? What will "they" think? are among the most frequent questions that assail the timid soul when it seeks to work for the Lord. At every turn this omnipotent and ubiquitous "they" stands in our way to discourage us and make us afraid. This form of discouragement is apt to come under the subtle disguise of a due consideration for the opinion of others; but it is especially dangerous, because it exalts this "they" into the place of God, and esteems "their" opinions above His promises. The only remedy here, as in all other forms of discouragement, is simply the reiteration of the fact that God is with us. "Be not afraid of their faces; for I am with thee to deliver thee, saith the Lord." "For he hath said, I will never leave thee nor forsake thee. So that we may boldly say, Thy Lord is my helper, and I will not fear what man shall do unto me." How can any heart, however timid, dare to indulge in discouragement in the face of such assertions as these?

There is, however, one sort of discouragement that is very common, and that seems as if it must be right, even though in all other cases it may be wrong, and that is the discouragement that arises from our own failures. It was from this sort of discouragement that the children of Israel suffered after their defeat at Ai. They had "committed a trespass in the accursed thing," and "therefore they could not stand before their enemies"; and so great was their discouragement that it is said, "wherefore the hearts of the people melted and became as water," and "Joshua rent his clothes, and fell to the earth upon his face before the ark of the Lord, until the eventide, he and all the elders of Israel, and put dust upon their heads." When God's own people "turn their backs before their enemies" one might well think they ought indeed to "lie on their faces," and "put dust on their heads," because of the dishonor they have brought upon His great name. Discouragement and despair would seem the only proper and safe condition after such failures. But evidently the Lord thought otherwise, for He said to Joshua, "Get thee up; wherefore liest thou upon thy face?" The proper thing to do after a failure is not to abandon ourselves to utter discouragement, humble as this may appear; but at once to face the evil, and get rid of it, and afresh and immediately to consecrate ourselves again to the Lord. "Up, sanctify yourselves," is always God's command. "Lie down and be discouraged" is always our temptation.

But you may ask whether a sense of sin produced by the convictions of the Holy Spirit ought not to cause discouragement. If I see myself to be a sinner, how can I help being discouraged? To this I answer that the Holy Spirit does not convict us of sin in order to discourage us, but to encourage us. His work is to show us our sin, not that we may lie down in despair under its power, but that we may get rid of it. A good mother points out the faults of her children for the purpose of helping them correct those faults; and the convictions of the Holy Spirit are in truth one of our greatest privileges, if we only had the sense to see it; for they mean, not that we are to give up in discouragement, but that we are to be encouraged to believe that deliverance is coming.

The good housewife discovers the stains on her table linen, not in order that she may have it thrown aside as no longer fit for use, but in order that she may have it cleansed for future use; and, if she has a good laundress, she will not be discouraged by the worst of stains. Surely then when God says to us, "Though your sins be as scarlet, they shall be as white as snow," it is pure unbelief on our part to allow ourselves to be discouraged at even the worst of our failures, for God's "washing of regeneration" must be at least as effectual as the washing of any human laundress could possibly be.

Fenelon says concerning this: "It is of great importance to guard against discouragement on account of our faults. Discouragement is not a fruit of humility, but of pride, and nothing can be worse. It springs from a secret love of our own excellence. We are hurt at feeling what we are. If we become discouraged we are the more enfeebled, and from our reflections on our own imperfections, a chagrin arises that is often worse than the imperfection itself. Poor nature longs from self-love to behold itself perfect; it is vexed that it is not so, it is impatient, haughty, and out of temper with itself and with everybody else. Sad state; as though the work of God could be accomplished by our ill-humor. As though the peace of God could be attained by our interior restlessness."

Discouragement, from whatever source it may come, produces many sad results. One of its very worst is that it leads people to "murmur," and to "speak against God." When the children of Israel were "discouraged because of the way," we are told that they "spake against God," and asked all sorts of God-dishonoring questions. And I believe, if we could examine the causes of the rebelling and murmuring thoughts that sometimes beset us, we could find that they always begin in discouragement. The truth is that discouragement is really, in its essence, a "speaking against God," for it necessarily implies some sort of a failure on His part to come up to that which His promises have led us to expect of Him. The psalmist recognizes this, and says concerning the discouraging questions His people asked in the days of their wilderness wandering, "Yes, they 'spake against God'; they said, 'Can God furnish a table in the wilderness?'" It appears, therefore, that even our questions as to God's power or willingness to help us, which perhaps seem to us so reasonable and even so humble, are really a "speaking against God," and are displeasing to Him, because they reveal the sad fact that we "believe not in him, and trust not in his salvation."

Another grievous quality in discouragement is its contagiousness. Nothing is more catching than discouragement. When the spies sent out by Moses brought up, as we have seen, and "evil report of the promised land," and told of the giants there, they so "discouraged the hearts of their brethren," that the people "lifted up their voices and cried," and utterly refused to go into the very land which the Lord had given them, and which they had started out to possess.

The "evil report" that so many Christians bring of their failures and their disappointments in the Christian life is one of the most discouraging things in our intercourse with one another. The hearts of many young Christians are, I believe, far too often thus discouraged by their older brethren, who have but little idea of the harm they are doing by their doleful accounts of the trials of the way.

I can never look back without shame to a time in my own life when I "discouraged the heart" of a young Christian friend, by the "evil report" I gave her of the "giants" of doubt and difficulty I had met with in my Christian pathway. And afterward, when a stronger faith in God had delivered me from all fear of these giants, I found that my former evil report had so effectually "discouraged her heart" that it was a long time before I could induce her to hearken to the good report I had then to bring.

So important did the Lord feel it to be that no one should discourage the heart of another that when Moses was giving to the Israelites God's laws concerning their methods of warfare, he said: "And the officers shall speak further unto the people, and they shall say, What man is there that is fearful and fainthearted? let him go and return unto his house, lest his brethren's heart faint as well as his heart."

Discouraged people, if they must be discouraged, ought at least to keep their discouragements to themselves, hidden away in the privacy of their own bosoms lest they should discourage the hearts of their brethren. We know from experience that courage is contagious, and that one really brave soul in moments of danger can save a crowd from a panic. But we too often fail to remember that the converse of this is true, and that one fainthearted man or woman can infect a whole crowd with fear. We consequently think nothing of expressing with the utmost freedom the foolish and wicked discouragements that are paralyzing all our own courage. We even sometimes, strange to say, sing our discouragements in our hymns at church or in prayer meeting.

*Where is the blessedness I knew*
*When first I saw the Lord?*
*Where is that soul-refreshing view*
*Of Jesus and His Word?*
*What peaceful hours I then enjoyed,*
*How sweet their memory still;*
*But now I find an aching void,*
*The world can never fill.*

Or this:

*And shall we then forever live*
*At this poor dying rate,*
*Our love so faint, so cold to thee,*
*And Thine to us so great?*

*In vain we tune our formal songs,*
*In vain we strive to rise;*
*Hosannas languish on our tongues,*
*And our devotion dies.*

To sing such hymns seems to me the greatest travesty on the worship of God that could well be conceived of. If there are "aching voids" in our experience, if our "love is cold and faint," and if we are living at a "poor, dying rate," at least let us keep it to ourselves. Because "hosannas languish on our tongues" is no reason why complainings and murmurings should be exalted into their place. Surely we cannot think it can be pleasing to God to hear them. What would we think of wives who should meet together to sing such things about their relation to their husbands? I do not believe they would be tolerated in society a single day.

If the church of Christ would only expurgate all the hymns of discouragement from its hymn books, and would allow none but hymns of courage and good cheer to be sung by its members, I believe the faith of Christians would go up with a mighty bound. "Be of good cheer" is the command of the Lord for His disciples, always and under all circumstances; and He founded this command on the tremendous fact that He had overcome the world, and that therefore there was nothing left for us to be discouraged about. As I have said before, if we only understood what it means that Christ has overcome the world, I believe we would be aghast at the very idea of any one of His followers ever being discouraged again.

If you had been an Israelite in those days, which would you rather have been, dear reader, the spies who brought an evil report of the land, and so discouraged the hearts of their brethren as to bring upon them the dreary forty years of wilderness wandering, or Caleb and Joshua, who "stilled the people before Moses, and said, Let us go up at once and possess the land; for we are well able to overcome it"?

Which will you be now?

In the divine review of this episode, Moses spoke of Caleb as one who had "wholly followed" the Lord; and this "wholly following" consisted simply and only in the fact that Caleb had given his brethren a good report of land, and, when his colleagues had made the heart of the people to melt by their evil report, had encouraged them to go up and possess it.

I hardly think that this is the general interpretation of what "wholly following" means; and I fear that many otherwise really devoted Christians fail in this essential point and seem to make it almost the principal mission of their lives to discourage the hearts of their brethren by the doleful and despairing reports they bring of the difficulties and dangers of the way.

How different it would be if discouragement were looked upon in its true light as a "speaking against God," and only encouraging words were permitted among Christians and encouraging reports heard! How many times would the children of Israel have failed in conquering their enemies had there been no men of faith among them to encourage and cheer them? And, on the other hand, who can tell how many spiritual defeats and disasters your discouragements, dear reader, may have brought about in your own life, and in the lives of those around you?

In one of Isaiah's prophecies which begins with, "Comfort ye, comfort ye my people, saith your God," he gives us a wonderful description of God as the ground of comfort, and then sets forth what His people ought to be; and says in the course of the latter: "They helped everyone his neighbor, and everyone said to his brother, Be of good courage. So the carpenter encouraged the goldsmith, and he that smootheth with the hammer him that smote the anvil."

Shall we follow their example, and from henceforth encourage one another instead of discouraging?

If I am asked how we are to get rid of discouragements, I can only say, as I have had to say of so many other wrong spiritual habits, we must give them up. It is never worth while to argue against discouragement. There is only one argument that can meet it, and that is the argument of God. When David was in the midst of what were perhaps the most discouraging moments of his life, when he had found his city burned, and his wives stolen, and he and the men with him had wept until they had no more power to weep; and when his men, exasperated at their misfortunes, spake of stoning him, then we are told, "But David encouraged himself in the Lord his God"; and the result was a magnificent victory, in which all that they had lost was more than restored to them. This always will be, and always must be the result of a courageous faith, because faith lays hold of the omnipotence of God.

Over and over the psalmist asks himself this question: "Why art thou cast down, O my soul, and why art thou disquieted within me?" And each time he answers himself with the argument of God: "Hope thou in God; for I shall yet praise him, who is the health of my countenance, and my God." He does not analyze his disquietude, or try to argue it away, but he turns at once to the Lord and by faith begins to praise Him.

It is the only way. Discouragement flies where faith appears; and, vice versa, faith flies when discouragement appears. We must choose between them, for they will not mix.

# Chapter Fourteen - The Shout of Faith

"And when ye hear the sound of the trumpet, all the people shall shout with a great shout; and the wall of the city shall fall down flat, and the people shall ascend up, every man straight before him."

The shout of a steadfast faith is an experience that is in direct contrast to the moans of a wavering faith, and to the wails of discouraged hearts, both of which we have been considering in our last two chapters. In the history of the children of Israel there were many occasions when they indulged in these moanings and wailings and always to their sad undoing; but on one occasion at least they gave a magnificent shout of steadfast faith that brought them a glorious victory. And among the many "secrets of the Lord" that are discovered by the soul in its onward progress, I do not know of any that is more practically valuable than the secret of this shout of faith.

The occasion when it took place was at the time when the Israelites had just crossed the River Jordan, and were about to take possession of the Promised Land. God had said to Joshua, just before they crossed: "Now therefore arise, go over this Jordan, thou, and all this people, unto the land which I do give to them, even to the children of Israel. Every place that the sole of your foot shall tread upon, that have I given unto you, as I said unto Moses."

With this warrant they had crossed the river and entered into the land, no doubt expecting to get immediate possession. But at once upon their entrance they were brought face to face with one of those "cities great and walled up to heaven" that had so discouraged the heart of the spies forty years before. Well might they be appalled at the sight of it. To the eye of sense there seemed no possibility that they could ever conquer Jericho. They had no engines of warfare with which to attack it; and one can easily imagine the despair that must have seized upon them when they found themselves confronted with the walls and fortresses of such a city.

But the Lord had said to Joshua: "See, I have given into thine hand Jericho, and the king thereof, and the mighty men of valor." He had not said, "I will give," but, "I have given." It belonged to them already; but now they were called upon to take possession of it. It was as if a king should bestow an estate upon a courtier who was away in a foreign land, and this courtier should come back to take possession of it.

But the great question was, How? It looked impossible. But the Lord declared His plan; and after a few directions as to the order of their march, and blowing of their trumpets, He closed with these strange words: "And it shall come to pass, that when they make a long blast with the ram's horn, and when ye hear the sound of the trumpet, all the people shall shout with a great shout; and the wall of the city shall fall down flat, and the people shall ascend up, every man straight before him" (Joshua 6:5).

Strange words but true, for it came to pass just as the Lord had said. On the seventh day, when the priests blew with the trumpets, Joshua said to the people, "Shout, for the Lord hath given you the city." "And it came to pass, when the people heard the sound of the trumpet, and the people shouted with a great shout, that the walls fell down flat, so that the people went up into the city, every man straight before him, and they took the city."

Now, no one can suppose for a moment that this shout caused the walls to fall. And yet the secret of their victory lay in just this shout. For it was the shout of a faith which dared, on the authority of God's Word alone, to claim a promised victory while as yet there were no signs of this victory being accomplished. And according to their faith God did unto them; so that, when they shouted, He made the walls to fall.

God had declared that He had given them the city, and faith reckoned this to be true. Unbelief might well have said, "It would be better not to shout until the walls do actually fall, for, should there be any failure about it, the men of Jericho will triumph, and we shall bring dishonor on the name of our God." But faith laughed at all such prudential considerations, and, confidently resting on God's Word, gave a shout of victory while yet to the eye of sense that victory seemed impossible. And long centuries afterward the Holy Ghost thus records this triumph of faith in Hebrews: "By faith the walls of Jericho fell down, after they were compassed about seven days."

*Faith, mighty faith, the promise sees*
*And looks at that alone;*
*Laughs at impossibilities,*
*And cries, It shall be done.*

Jehoshaphat is another example of this shout of faith. He was told that a great multitude was coming up against him from beyond the sea, and he realized that he and his people had "no might" against them, and he could not tell "what to do." He did not waste his time and his energies in trying to prepare engines of warfare or in arranging plans for a battle, but he at once "set himself to seek the Lord." He stood in the congregation of the people, and said: "O Lord God of our fathers, art not thou God in heaven? and rulest not thou over all the kingdoms of the heathen? And in thine hand is there not power and might, so that none is able to withstand thee? Art not thou our God, who didst drive out the inhabitants of this land before thy people Israel, and gavest it to the seed of Abraham, thy friend, forever?... And now behold, the children of Ammon and Moab and Mount Seir ... come to cast us out of thy possession, which thou hast given us to inherit. O our God, wilt thou not judge them? For we have no might against this great company that cometh against us; neither know we what to do: but our eyes are upon thee."

To this appeal the Lord answered through the mouth of His prophet in the following words: "Thus saith the Lord unto you, Be not afraid nor dismayed by reason of this great multitude, for the battle is not yours but God's ... Ye shall not need to fight in this battle; set yourselves, stand ye still, and see the salvation of the Lord with you. O Judah and Jerusalem, fear not, nor be dismayed; tomorrow go out against them; for the Lord will be with you."

Without a thought of doubt Jehoshaphat and the children of Israel believed the Word of the Lord and began at once to praise Him beforehand for the victory that they were sure was coming. The next morning they rose early and went out to meet their enemy; and Jehoshaphat, instead of exhorting them as an ordinary general would have done to look to their arms and to be brave in battle, simply called upon them to have a courageous faith. "Hear me, O Judah, and ye inhabitants of Jerusalem," he said, "believe in the Lord your God, so shall ye be established; believe his prophets, so shall ye prosper."

Jehoshaphat then consulted with the people; and as their faith proved equal to his own, they appointed singers to go out before the army to sing praises as they went forward to meet the enemy. And it came to pass that when they began to sing and to praise, the Lord began to set ambushments against the enemy, so that they smote one another; and when the children of Israel came to a watchtower in the wilderness, from which they could see the great multitude that had come up against them, "behold, they were dead bodies fallen to the earth, and none escaped."

By this wonderful method of warfare they were made even "more than conquerors"; for they were "three days in gathering the spoil, it was so much."

David's fight with Goliath is another example of this method of victory. To the eye of sense David had no chance whatever of conquering the mighty giant, who had been defying the armies of Israel. But David, looking with the eye of faith, could see the unseen divine forces that were fighting on his side, and when Saul said to him: "Thou art not able to go against this Philistine to fight with him, for thou art but a youth, and he a man of war from his youth," David stood firm in his faith; and, after recounting some of his past deliverances, said calmly: "The Lord that delivered me out of the paw of the lion, and out of the paw of the bear, he will deliver me out of the hand of this Philistine." Saul, partly convinced by this strong faith, said, "Go, and the Lord be with thee." He could not, however, quite give up all trust in his own accustomed armor, and he armed David with a helmet of brass, and a coat of mail, and his own powerful sword, and David "assayed to go." But David soon found that he would not be able to fight in this sort of armor, and he put it off, and took instead the simple weapons that the Lord had blessed before—his staff, and his sling, and five smooth stones out of the brook; and thus equipped, he drew near to the giant.

When the giant saw the stripling who had come to fight him, he disdained him, and said contemptuously: "Come to me, and I will give thy flesh to the fowls of the air and the beasts of the field." And truly to the eye of the sense it looked as though this must necessarily be the end of such an apparently unequal battle. But David's faith triumphed, and he shouted a shout of victory before even the battle had begun. "Thou comest to me," he said, "with a sword, and with a spear, and with a shield; but I come to thee in the name of the Lord of hosts, the God of the armies of Israel, whom thou defiest. This day will the Lord deliver thee into mine hand, and I will smite thee, and take thy head from thee ... that all the earth may know that there is a God in Israel. And all this assembly shall know that the Lord saveth not with sword and spear: for the battle is the Lord's, and he will give you into our hands."

In the face of such faith as this, what could even a giant do? Every word of that triumphant shout of victory was fulfilled; and the mighty enemy was delivered into the hands of the stripling he had disdained.

And so it will always be. Nothing can withstand the triumphant faith that links itself to omnipotence. For "this is the victory that overcometh the world, even our faith."

The secret of all successful warfare lies in this shout of faith. It is a secret incomprehensible to those who know nothing of the unseen divine power that waits on the demands of faith; a secret that must always seem, to those who do not understand it, the height of folly and imprudence.

We are all called to be "good soldiers of Jesus Christ," and to fight the "good fight of faith" against worse enemies than those which attacked the Israelites. Our enemies are interior, and the giant that defies us is the strength of our temptations and the powerlessness of our own strength to resist. It is a hard, and often a very discouraging fight, and many of God's children are weighed down under a dreary sense of apparently hopeless failure. They have sinned and repented again, so often, that they can see no hope of victory, and are ready to despair. They hate sin, and they love righteousness, and they long for victory, but the good that they would they do not, and the evil that they would not that they do. In the language of the apostle they find a law in their members warring against the law of their mind, and bringing them into captivity to the law of sin that is in their members. They know they ought to conquer, but they do not know how. And it is for these that this chapter is written. If they can but discover the secret of this shout of faith they will know how, for it is absolutely certain that it never fails to bring victory.

In John 16:33 our Lord reveals the ground of this triumphant shout of faith. “Be of good cheer,” He says, “for I have overcome the world.” Not “I will overcome,” but “I have overcome.” It is already done; and nothing remains but for us to enter into the power of it. Joshua did not say to the people, “Shout, for the Lord will give you the city,” but “Shout, for he hath given it.” It has always seemed to me that it must have drained all Joshua’s will power to his lips to render it possible for him to make such a statement, in face of the fact that the walls of the city were at that very minute standing up as massive and as impregnable as ever. But God was a reality to Joshua, and he was not afraid to proclaim the victory that had been promised, even before it was accomplished.

There is a great difference between saying, “The Lord will give,” and “The Lord hath given.” A victory promised in the future may be hindered or prevented by a thousand contingencies, but a victory already accomplished cannot be gainsaid. And when our Lord assures us, not that He will overcome the world, but that He has already done so, He gives an assured foundation for a shout of the most triumphant victory. Henceforward the forces of sin are a defeated and demoralized foe; and, if we believe the words of Christ, we can meet them without fear, since we have been made more than conquerors through Him who loves us.

It is a well-known fact that as long as a defeated army can keep its defeat a secret, it can still make some show of resistance. But the moment it finds out that its defeat is known, it loses all heart and becomes utterly demoralized, and has no resource left but to retreat.

The secret then lies in this that we must meet sin, not as a foe that has yet to be conquered, but as one that has already been conquered. When Rahab helped the spies who had been sent by Joshua to escape from the king of Jericho, she made this confession: “I know that the Lord hath given you the land, and that your terror is fallen upon us, and that all the inhabitants of the land faint because of you.” If we were gifted with eyes that could see the unseen kingdom of evil, I believe we also should find that a terror and faintness has fallen upon all the forces of that unknown region, and that they see in every man and woman of faith a sure and triumphant conqueror.

It is because we do not know this secret that we meet our spiritual enemies with such fear and trembling, and suffer such disastrous defeats.

A Christian I know, who had been fearfully beset by temptation against which she had seemed to struggle in vain, was told this secret by one who had discovered it. It brought conviction at once, and she went forth to a fresh battle with the assurance of an already accomplished victory. It is needless to say that she was victorious; and she said afterward that it seemed to her as if she could almost hear the voice of the tempter saying as he slunk away, "Alas! it is all up with me now. She had found out the secret. She knows that I am an already conquered foe, and I am afraid I shall never be able to overcome her again!"

We are told that "for this purpose the Son of God was manifested, that he might destroy the works of the devil"; and again: "Ye know that he was manifested to take away our sins; and in him is no sin"; and again: "Now once in the end of the world hath he appeared to put away sin by the sacrifice of himself." We must accept it as a fact, therefore, that sin is for us a conquered foe. And if our faith will only lay hold of this fact, reckoning sin to be dead to us, and ourselves to be dead to sin; and will dare, when we come in sight of temptation, to raise the shout of victory, we shall surely find as the Israelites did that every wall will fall down flat, and that a pathway will be opened straight before us to take the city!

Our enemies are giants now just as truly as they were in Israel's day; and cities as great as Jericho, with walls as high, confront us in our heavenly pathway. Like the Israelites of old, we have no human weapons with which to conquer them. Our armor, like theirs, must be the "armor of God." Our shield is the same invisible shield of faith that protected them; and our sword must be, as theirs was, the sword of the Spirit which is the Word, that is, the promises and declarations of God. When our faith puts on this "armor of God," and lays hold of this "sword of the Spirit," and we confront our enemy with a shout of undaunted faith, we cannot fail to conquer the mightiest giant, or to take the strongest city.

But alas! how different is the usual method of our Christian warfare. Instead of a triumphant shout of victory, we meet our temptations with feeble resolutions, or with futile arguments, or with halfhearted self-upbraiding, or, failing all else, with despairing prayers. "O Lord, save me!" we cry; "O Lord, deliver me!" And when no deliverance has come, and the temptation has swept aside all our arguments and all our resolutions, and we have been grievously defeated, then we have cried out in our despair that God has failed us, and that there is for us no truth in the apostle's declaration that with every temptation there is a way of escape that we may be able to bear it. This is the usual and the unsuccessful way of meeting temptation, as many of us know to our cost. But what we ought to do is very different. We must recognize it as a fact that sin is a conquered foe, and must meet it, therefore, with a shout of victory instead of with a cry for help. Where we prayed that the Lord would save us, we must make now the assertion that He does save us, and that he saves us now. We must add the little letter s to the word save, and make it the present instead of the future tense.

The walls may look as high and as immovable as ever; and prudence may say it is not safe to shout until the victory is actually won. But the faith that can shout in the midst of the sorest stress of temptation, "Jesus saves me; He saves me now!"

such a faith will be sure to win a glorious and a speedy victory. Many of God's children have tried this plan, and have found it to work far beyond even their expectations. Temptations have come in upon them like a flood—temptations to irritability, or to wicked thoughts, or to bitterness of spirit, or to a thousand other things, and they have seen their danger; and their fears and their feelings have declared that there was no hope of escape. But their faith has laid hold of this grand fact that Christ has conquered; and they have fixed their gaze on the unseen power of God's salvation, and have given their shout of victory, "The Lord saves! He saves me now! I am more than conqueror through Him that loves me!" And the result is always a glorious victory.

It may sometimes seem so impossible that the Lord can or does save that the words will not say themselves inside, but have to be said aloud, forcing one's lips to utter them over and over, shutting one's eyes and closing one's ears against every suggestion of doubt no matter how plausible it may seem. These declarations of faith often seem untrue at first, so apparently real are the seen reasons for doubt and discouragement. But the unseen facts are truer than the seen, and if the faith that lays hold of them is steadfastly persisted in, they never fail in the end to prove themselves to be the very truth of God. "According to our faith" it always must be unto us, sooner or later, and when we shout the shout of faith, the Lord invariably gives the victory of faith.

I knew a Christian man who had entered upon this life of faith. He had naturally a violent temper and went about his work among his ungodly companions was sorely beset with temptations to give way to it. He knew it was wrong, and he struggled valiantly against it, but all in vain. Finally, one morning on his way to work he called in despair at the house of his Christian teacher and told him his difficulties. After explaining the suddenness of the temptations that came upon him, and the lack of time even to pray for help before he was overcome, he said, "Now can you tell me of any short road to victory; something that I can lay hold of just at the needed moment?"

"Yes," replied the minister; "when the temptation comes, at once lift up your heart to the Lord, and by faith claim the promised victory. Shout the shout of faith, and the temptation will flee before you."

After a little explanation of the glorious fact that sin is an already conquered foe, the man seemed to understand and went on his way to take his place in the ranks with his fellow men at the station where they were engaged in hauling freight. As usual he was met by taunts and sneers; and in addition he found that they had jostled him out of his rightful place in the ranks. The temptation to anger was almost overwhelming, but, folding his arms, he said inwardly over and over, "Jesus saves me; He saves me now!" At once his heart was filled with peace, and the victory was complete. Again he was tried; a heavy box was so rolled as to fall on his foot badly injuring him, and again he folded his arms and repeated his shout of victory, and at once all was calm. And so the day passed on. Trials and temptations abounded, but his triumphant shout carried him safely through them all, and the fiery darts of the enemy were all quenched by the shield of faith which he continually lifted up. Nighttime found him more than conqueror through Him who loved him; and even his fellow carmen were forced to own the reality and the beauty of a religion that could so triumph over their aggravating assaults.

The psalmist, after telling of the enemies who were daily trying to swallow him up, declared triumphantly: "When I cry unto thee, then shall mine enemies turn back: this I know; for God is for me."

Dear reader, do you know what the psalmist knew? Do you know that God is for you, and that He will cause your enemies to turn back? If you do, then go out to meet your temptations, singing a song of triumph as you go. Meet your very next temptation in this way. At this first approach begin to give thanks for the victory. Claim continually that you are more than conqueror through Him that loves you, and refuse to be daunted by any foe. Shout the shout of faith with Joshua, and Jehoshaphat, and David, and Paul; and I can assure you that when you shout, the Lord will "set ambushments," and all your enemies shall fall down dead before you.

# Chapter Fifteen - Thanksgiving Versus Complaining

"In everything give thanks, for this is the will of God in Christ Jesus concerning you."

Thanksgiving or complaining—these words express two contrastive attitudes of the souls of God's children in regard to His dealings with them; and they are more powerful than we are inclined to believe in furthering or frustrating His purposes of comfort and peace toward us. The soul that gives thanks can find comfort in everything; the soul that complains can find comfort in nothing.

God's command is "In everything give thanks"; and the command is emphasized by the declaration, "for this is the will of God in Christ Jesus concerning you." It is an actual positive command; and if we want to obey God, we have simply got to give thanks in everything. There is no getting around it.

But a great many Christians have never realized this; and, although they may be familiar with the command, they have always looked upon it as a sort of counsel of perfection to which mere flesh and blood could never be expected to attain. And they, unconsciously to themselves perhaps, change the wording of the passage to make it say "be resigned" instead of "give thanks," and "in a few things" instead of "in everything," and they leave out altogether the words, "for this is the will of God in Christ Jesus concerning you."

If brought face to face with the actual wording of the command, such Christians will say, "Oh, but it is an impossible command. If everything came direct from God, one might do it perhaps, but most things come through human sources, and often are the result of sin, and it would not be possible to give thanks for these." To this I answer that it is true we cannot always give thanks for the things themselves, but we can always give thanks for God's love and care in the things. He may not have ordered them, but He is in them somewhere, and He is in them to compel, even the most grievous, to work together for our good.

The "second causes" of the wrong may be full of malice and wickedness, but faith never sees second causes. It sees only the hand of God behind the second causes. They are all under His control, and not one of them can touch us except with His knowledge and permission. The thing itself that happens cannot perhaps be said to be the will of God, but by the time its effects reach us they have become God's will for us, and must be accepted as from His hands.

The story of Joseph is an illustration of this. Nothing could have seemed more entirely an act of sin, nor more utterly contrary to the will of God than his being sold to the Ishmaelites by his wicked brethren; and it would not have seemed possible for Joseph, when he was being carried off into slavery in Egypt, to give thanks. And yet, if he had known the end from the beginning, he would have been filled with thanksgiving. The fact of his having been sold into slavery was the direct doorway to the greatest triumphs and blessings of his life. And, at the end, Joseph himself could say to his wicked brethren: "As for you, ye thought evil against me, but God meant it unto good." To the eye of sense it was Joseph's wicked brethren who had sent him into Egypt, but Joseph, looking at it with the eye of faith, said, "God did send me."

We can all remember, I think, similar instances in our own lives when God has made the wrath of man to praise Him, and has caused even the hardest trails to work together for our greatest good. I recollect once in my own life when a trial was brought upon me by another person, at which I was filled with bitter rebellion and could not see in it from beginning to end anything to be thankful for. But, as it was in the case of Joseph, that very trial worked out for me the richest blessings and the greatest triumphs of my whole life; and in the end I was filled with thanksgiving for the very things that had caused me such bitter rebellion before. If only I had had faith enough to give thanks at first, how much sorrow would have been spared me.

But I am afraid that the greatest heights to which most Christians in their shortsightedness seem able to rise is to strive after resignation to things they cannot alter, and to seek for patience to endure them. And the result is that thanksgiving is almost an unknown exercise among the children of God; and, instead of giving thanks in everything, many of them hardly give thanks in anything. If the truth were told, Christians as a body must be acknowledged to be but a thankless set. It is considered in the world a very discourteous thing for one man to receive benefits from another man and fail to thank him, and I cannot see why it is not just as discourteous a thing not to thank God. And yet we find people who would not for the world omit an immediate note of thanks upon the reception of any gift, however trifling, from a human friend, but who have never given God real thanks for any one of the innumerable benefits He has been showering upon them all their long lives.

Moreover, I am afraid a great many not only fail to give thanks, but they do exactly the opposite, and allow themselves instead to complain and murmur about God's dealings with them. Instead of looking out for His goodness, they seem to delight in picking out His shortcomings, and think they show a spirit of discernment in criticizing His laws and His ways. We are told that "when the people complained, it displeased the Lord"; but we are tempted to think that our special complaining, because it is spiritual complaining, cannot displease Him since it is a pious sort of complaining, and is a sign of greater zeal on our part, and of deeper spiritual insight than is possessed by the ordinary Christian.

But complaining is always alike, whether it is on the temporal or the spiritual plane. It always has in it the element of fault-finding. Webster says to complain means to make a charge or an accusation. It is not merely disliking the thing we have to bear, but it contains the element of finding fault with the agency that lies behind it. And if we will carefully examine the true inwardness of our complainings, I think we shall generally find they are founded on a subtle fault-finding with God. We secretly feel as if He were to blame somehow; and, almost unconsciously to ourselves, we make mental charges against Him.

On the other hand, thanksgiving always involves praise of the giver. Have you ever noticed how much we are urged in the Bible to "praise the Lord"? It seemed to be almost the principal part of the worship of the Israelites. "Praise ye the Lord, for the Lord is good: sing praises to his name, for it is pleasant." This is the continual refrain of everything all through the Bible. I believe, if we should count up, we would find that there are more commands given and more examples set for the giving of thanks "always for all things" than for the doing or the leaving undone of anything else.

It is very evident from the whole teaching of Scripture that the Lord loves to be thanked and praised just as much as we like it. I am sure that it gives Him real downright pleasure, just as it does us; and that our failure to thank Him for His "good and perfect gifts" wounds His loving heart, just as our hearts are wounded when our loved ones fail to appreciate the benefits we have so enjoyed bestowing upon them. What a joy it is to us to receive from our friends an acknowledgment of their thanksgiving for our gifts, and is it no likely that it is a joy to the Lord also?

When the apostle is exhorting the Ephesian Christians to be "followers of God as dear children," one of the exhortations he gives in connection with being filled with the Spirit is this: "Giving thanks always for all things unto God and the Father, in the name of our Lord Jesus Christ." "Always for all things" is a very sweeping expression, and it is impossible to suppose it can be whittled down to mean only the few and scanty thanks, which seem all that many Christians manage to give. It must mean, I am sure, that there can be nothing in our lives which has not in it somewhere a cause for thanksgiving, and that, no mater who or what may be the channel to convey it, everything contains for us a hidden blessing from God.

The apostle tells us that "every creature of God is good, and nothing to be refused, if it be received with thanksgiving." But it is very hard for us to believe things are good when they do not look so. Often the things God sends into our lives look like curses instead of blessings; and those who have no eyes that can see below surfaces judge by the outward seemings only and never see the blessed realities beneath.

How many "good and perfect gifts" we must have had during our lives, which we have looked upon only as curses, and for which we have never returned one thought of thanks! And for how many gifts also, which we have even acknowledged to be good, have we thanked ourselves, or our friends, or our circumstances, without once looking behind the earthly givers to thank the heavenly Giver, from whom in reality they all come! It is as if we should thank the messengers who bring us our friends' gifts, but should never send any word of thanks to our friends themselves.

But, even when we realize that things come directly from God, we find it very hard to give thanks for what hurts us. Do we not, however, all know what it is to thank a skillful physician for his treatment of our diseases, even though that treatment may have been very severe. And surely we should no less give thanks to our divine Physician, when He is obliged to give us bitter medicine to cure our spiritual diseases, or to perform a painful operation to rid us of something that harms.

But instead of thanking Him we complain against Him; although we generally direct our complaints, not against the divine Physician himself who has ordered our medicine, but against the "bottle" in which He has sent it. This "bottle" is usually some human being, whose unkindness or carelessness, or neglect, or cruelty has caused our suffering; but who has been after all only the instrumentality or "second cause" that God has used for our healing.

Good common sense tells us that it would be folly to rail against the bottles in which the medicines, prescribed by our earthy physicians, come to us; and it is equal folly to rail against the "second causes" that are meant to teach us the lessons our souls need to learn.

When the children of Israel found themselves wandering in the wilderness, they "murmured against Moses and Aaron," and complained that they had brought them forth into the wilderness to kill them with hunger. But in reality their complaining was against God, for it was really He who had brought them there, and not Moses and Aaron, who were only the "second causes." And the psalmist in recounting the story afterward called this murmuring against Moses and Aaron a "speaking against God." Divine history takes no account of second causes, but goes directly to the real cause behind them.

We may settle it, therefore, that all complaining is at the bottom "speaking against God," whether we are conscious of it or not. We may think, as the Israelites did, that our discomforts and deprivations have come from human hands only, and may therefore feel at liberty to "murmur against" the second causes which have, we may think, brought about our trials. But God is the great Cause behind all second causes. The second causes are only the instrumentalities that He uses; and when we murmur against these, we are really murmuring, not against the instrumentalities, but against God Himself. Second causes are powerless to act, except by God's permission; and what He permits becomes really His arranging. The psalmist tells us that when the Lord heard the complainings of His people "He was wroth," and His anger came up against them "because they believed not in God, and trusted not in his salvation." And, at the bottom, all complainings mean just this, that we do not believe in God, and do not trust in His salvation.

The psalmist says: "I will praise the name of God with a song, and magnify him with thanksgiving. This also shall please the Lord better than an ox or bullock that hath horns and hoofs." A great many people seem quite ready and willing to offer up an "ox or a bullock," or some great sacrifice to the Lord, but never seem to have realized that a little genuine praise and thanksgiving offered to Him now and then would "please him better" than all their great sacrifices made in His cause.

As I said before, the Bible is full of this thought from beginning to end. Over and over it is called a "sacrifice of thanksgiving," showing that it is as really an act of religious worship, as is any other religious act. In fact, the "sacrifice of thanksgiving" was one of the regular sacrifices ordained by God in the Book of Leviticus. "Oh that men would praise the Lord for his goodness, and for his wonderful works to the children of men! And let them sacrifice the sacrifices of thanksgiving, and declare his works with rejoicing." By Him, therefore, let us offer the sacrifice of praise to God continually, that is, the fruit of our lips, giving thanks to His name.

It is such an easy thing to offer the "sacrifice of thanksgiving," that one would suppose everybody would be keen to do it. But somehow the contrary seems to be the case; and if the prayers of Christians were all to be noted down for any one single day, I fear it would be found that with them, as it was with the ten lepers who had been cleansed, nine out of every ten had offered no genuine thanks at all. Our Lord Himself was grieved at these ungrateful lepers, and said: "Were there not ten cleansed? But where are the nine? There are not found that returned to give glory to God, save this stranger." Will He have to ask the same question regarding any of us? We have often, it may be, wondered at the ingratitude of those nine cleansed lepers; but what about our own ingratitude? Do we not continually pass by blessings innumerable without notice, and instead fix our eyes on what we feel to be our trials and our losses, and think and talk about these, until our whole horizon is filled with them, and we almost begin to think we have no blessings at all?

We can judge of how this must grieve the Lord by our own feelings. A child who complains about the provision the parent has made wounds that parent's heart often beyond words. Some people are always complaining, nothing ever pleases them, and no kindness seems ever to be appreciated. We know how uncomfortable the society of such people makes us; and we know, on the contrary, how life is brightened by the presence of one who never complains, but who finds something to be pleased with in all that comes. I believe far more misery than we imagine is caused in human hearts by the grumblings of those they love; and I believe also that woundings we never dream of, are given to the heart of our Father in Heaven by the continual murmuring of His children.

How often is it despairingly said of fretful, complaining spirits upon whom every care and attention has been lavished, "Will nothing ever satisfy them?" And how often must God turn away, grieved by our complainings, when His love has been lavished upon us in untold blessings. I have sometimes thought that if we could but realize this, we would check our inordinate grief over even the trials that come from the death of those we love, and would try, for His dear sake, to be cheerful and content even in our lonely and bereft condition.

I remember hearing of a dear girl who was obliged to undergo a serious and very painful treatment for some disease, and the doctors had dreaded the thought of her groans and outcries. But to their amazement not even a moan escaped her lips, and all the time she smiled at her father who was present, and uttered only words of love and tenderness. The doctors could not understand it, and when the worst was over one of them asked how it could have been. "Ah," she said, "I knew how much my father loved me, and I knew how he would suffer if he saw that I suffered, so I tried to hide my suffering; and I smiled to make him think I did not mind."

Can any of us do this for our heavenly Father?

Job was a great complainer; and we may perhaps think, as we read his story, that if ever anyone had good cause for complaining, he had. His circumstances seemed to be full of hopeless misery. "My soul is weary of my life; I will leave my complaint upon myself; I will speak in the bitterness of my soul. I will say unto God, Do not condemn me; show me wherefore thou contendest with me. Is it good unto thee that thou shouldest oppress, that thou shouldest despise the work of thine hands?"

We can hardly wonder at Job's complaint. And yet could he but have seen the divine side of all his troubles, he would have known that they were permitted in the tenderest love, and were to bring him a revelation of God such as he could have had by no other means. Could he have seen that this was to be the outcome he would not have uttered a single complaint, but would have given triumphant thanks for the trials which were to bring him such a glorious fruition. And could we but see, in our heaviest trials, the end from the beginning, I am sure that thanksgiving would take the place of complaining in every case.

The children of Israel were always complaining about something. They complained because they had no water; and when water was supplied they complained that it was bitter to their taste. And we likewise complain because the spiritual water we have to drink seems bitter to our taste. Our souls are athirst, and we do not like the supply that seems to be provided. Our experiences do not quench our thirst, our religious exercises seem dull and unsatisfying; we feel ourselves to be in a dry and thirsty land where no water is. We have turned from the "Fountain of living waters," and then we complain because the cisterns we have hewed out for ourselves hold no water.

The Israelites complained about their food. They had so little confidence in God that they were afraid they would die of starvation; and then when the heavenly manna was provided they complained again because they "loathed such light food." And we also complain about our spiritual food. Like the Israelites, we have so little confidence in God that we are always afraid we shall die of spiritual starvation. We complain because our preacher does not feed us, or because our religious privileges are very scanty, or because we are not supplied with the same spiritual fare as others are, who seem to us more highly favored; and we covet their circumstances or their experiences. We have asked God to feed us, and then our souls "loathe" the food He gives, and we think it is too "light" to sustain or strengthen us. We have asked for bread, and we complain that He has given a stone.

But, if we only knew it, the provision our divine Master has made of spiritual drink and spiritual food is just that which is best for us, and is that for which we would be the most thankful if we knew. The amazing thing is that we cannot believe now, without waiting for the end, that the Shepherd knows what pasture is best for His sheep. Surely if we did, our hearts would be filled with thanksgiving and our mouths with praise even in the wilderness.

Jonah was a wonderful illustration of this. His prayer of thanksgiving out of the "belly of hell" is a tremendous lesson. "I have cried by reason of mine affliction unto the Lord, and he heard me; out of the belly of hell cried I, and thou heardest my voice. For thou hadst cast me into the deep, in the midst of the sea: and the floods compassed me about; all thy billows and thy waves passed over me ... But I will sacrifice unto thee with a voice of thanksgiving; I will pay that I have vowed. Salvation is of the Lord."

No depth of misery, not even the "belly of hell," is too great for the sacrifice of thanksgiving. We cannot, it is true, give thanks for the misery, but we can give thanks to the Lord in the misery, just as Jonah did. No matter what our trouble, the Lord is in it somewhere; and, of course, being there, He is there to help and bless us. Therefore, when our "souls faint within us" because of our troubles, we have only to remember this, and to thank Him for His presence and His love.

It is not because things are good that we are to thank the Lord, but because He is good. We are not wise enough to judge as to things, whether they are really, in their essence, joys or sorrows. But we always know that the Lord is good, and that His goodness makes it absolutely certain that everything He provides or permits must be good; and must therefore be something for which we would be heartily thankful, if only we could see it with His eyes.

In a little tract called "Mrs. Pickett's Missionary Box," a poor woman, who had never done anything but complain all her life long, and who, consequently, had got to thinking that she had no benefits for which to give thanks, received a missionary box with the words written on it: "What shall I render unto the Lord for all His benefits toward me?" And she was asked by her niece, who believed in being thankful, to put a penny into the box for every benefit she could discover in her life. I will let her tell her own story.

" 'Great benefits I have!' says I, standing with my arms akimbo, an' lookin' that box all over. 'Guess the heathen won't get much out of me at that rate.' an' I jest made up my mind I would keep count, jest to show myself how little I did have. 'Them few pennies won't break me,' I thought, and I really seemed to kinder enjoy thinkin' over the hard times I had.

"Well, the box sat there all that week, an' I used to say it must be kinder lonesome with nothin' in it; for not a penny went into it until next missionary meetin' day. I was sittin' on the back steps gettin' a breath of fresh air, when Mary came home, an' sat down alongside o' me an' began to tell me about the meetin', an' it was all about Injy an' the widders there, poor creturs, an' they bein' abused, an' starved, an' not let to think for themselves—you know all about it better'n I do!—an' before I thought I up an' said-

" 'Well, if I be a widder, I'm thankful I'm where I kin earn my own livin', an' no thanks to nobody, an' no one to interfere!'

"Then Mary, she laughed an' said there was my fust benefit. Well, that sorter tickled me, for I thought a woman must be pretty hard up for benefits when she had to go clear off to Injy to find them, an' I dropped in one penny, an' it rattled round a few days without any company. I used to shake it every time I passed the shelf, an' the thought of them poor things in Injy kep' a comin' up before me, an' I really was glad when I got a new boarder for me best room, an' felt as if I'd oughter put in another. An' next meetin', Mary she told me about China, an' I thought about that till I put in another because I warn't a Chinese. An' all the while I felt kinder proud of how little there was in that box. Then one day, when I got a chance to turn a little penny sellin' eggs, which I warn't in the habit of, Mary brought the box in, where I was countin' of my money, and says-

" 'A penny for your benefit, Aunt Mirandy.'

"An' I says, 'This ain't the Lord's benefit.'

"An' she answered, 'If 'tain't His, whose is it?' An' she begun to hum over somethin' out of one of the poetry books that she was always a readin' of-

'God's grace is the only grace, And all grace is the grace of God.'

"Well, I dropped in my penny, an' them words kep' ringin' in my ears, till I couldn't help puttin' more to it, on account of some other things I never thought of callin' the Lord's benefits before. An' by that time, what with Mary's tellin' me about them meetin's, an' me most always findin' somethin' to put in a penny for, to be thankful that I warn't it, an' what with gettin' interested about it all, and sorter searchin' round a little now and then to think of somethin' or other to put a penny in for, there really come to be quite a few pennies in the box, an' it didn't ralle near so much when I shook it."

There is a psalm which I call our Benefit Psalm. It is Psalm 103, and it recounts some of the benefits the Lord has bestowed upon us, and urges us not to forget them. "Bless the Lord, O my soul, and forget not all his benefit." Our dear sister's Benefit Box had taught her something of the meaning of this psalm. All her life she had been forgetting the benefits the Lord had bestowed upon her, but now she was beginning to remember them.

Have we begun to remember ours?

If during the past year we had kept count of those benefits for which we had actually given thanks, how many pennies, I wonder, would our boxes have contained?

We sometimes sing at mission meetings a hymn of thanksgiving, with the chorus, "Count your many blessings, name them one by one, and it will surprise you what the Lord has done." And sometimes I have wondered whether any of us who were singing it so heartily had ever kept the slightest record of our blessings, or even in fact knew that we had any.

For the trouble is that very often God's gifts come to us wrapped up in such rough coverings that we are tempted to reject them as worthless; or the messengers who bring them come in the guise of enemies, and we want to shut the door against them, and not give them entrance. But we lose far more than we know when we reject even the most unlikely.

*Evil is only the slave of good,*
*And sorrow the servant of joy:*
*And the soul is mad that refuses food*
*From the meanest in God's employ.*

We are commanded to enter into His gates with thanksgiving, and into His courts with praise, and I am convinced that the giving of thanks is the key that opens these gates more quicky than anything else. Try it, dear reader. The next time you feel dead, cold, and low-spirited begin to praise and thank the Lord. Enumerate to yourself the benefits He has bestowed upon you, thank Him heartily for each one, and see if your spirits do not begin to rise, and your heart get warmed up.

Sometimes it may be that you feel too disheartened to pray; then try giving thanks instead; and, before you know it, you will find yourself "glad" in the multitude of His loving-kindnesses and His tender mercies.

One of my friends told me that her little boy one night flatly refused to say his prayers. He said there was not a single thing in all the world he wanted, and he did not see what was the good of asking for things that he did not want. A happy thought came to his mother as she said, "Well, Charlie, suppose then we give thanks for all the things you have got." The idea pleased the child, and he very willingly knelt down and began to give thanks. He thanked God for his marbles, and for a new top that had just been given him, and for his strong legs that could run so fast, and that he was not blind like a little boy he knew, and for his kind father and mother, and for his nice bed, and for one after another of his blessings, until the list grew so long that at last he said he believed he would never get done. And when finally they rose from their knees, he said to his mother, with his face shining with happiness, "Oh, Mother, I never knew before how perfectly splendid God is!" And I believe, if we sometimes followed the example of this little boy, we too would find out, as never before, the goodness of our God.

It is very striking to notice how much thanksgiving had to do with the building of the Temple. When they had collected the treasures for the Temple. When they had collected the treasures for the Temple, David gave thanks to the Lord for enabling them to do it. When the Temple was finished, they gave thanks again. And then a wonderful thing happened, for it came to pass as the trumpeters and singers were as one to make one sound to be heard in praising and thanking the Lord ... that then the house was filled with a cloud, even the house of the Lord, so that the priests could not stand to minister by reason of the cloud; for the glory of the Lord had filled the house of God. When the people praised and gave thanks, then the house was filled with the glory of the Lord. And we may be sure that the reason our hearts are not oftener filled with the "glory of the Lord" is because we do not often enough make our voices to be heard in praising and thanking Him.

If the giving of thanks is the way to open the gates of the Lord, complaining on the other hand closes these gates. Jude quotes a prophecy of Enoch's concerning murmurers: "The Lord cometh," he says, "to execute judgment upon all, and to convince all that are ungodly among them ... of all their hard speeches which ungodly sinners have spoken against him. These are murmurers, complainers, walking after their own lusts."

People who are "murmurers" and "complainers" make in their complainings more "hard speeches" against the Lord than they would like to own, or than they will care at the last day to face. And it is not to be wondered that the judgment of God, instead of the "glory of God," is the result.

I wish I had room to quote all the passages in the Bible about giving thanks and praises to the Lord. It is safe to say that there are hundreds and hundreds of them; and it is an amazing thing how they can have been so persistently ignored. I beg of you to read the last seven psalms, and see what you think. They are simply full to overflowing with a list of the things for which the psalmist calls upon us to give thanks; all of them are things relating to the character and the ways of God, which we dare not dispute. They are not for the most part private blessings of our own, but are the common blessings that belong to all humanity, and that contain within themselves every private blessing we can possibly need. But they are blessings which we continually forget, because we take them for granted, hardly noticing their existence, and never give thanks for them.

But the psalmist knew how to count his many blessings and name them one by one, and he would have us to do likewise. Try it, dear reader, and you will indeed be surprised to see what the Lord has done. Go over these psalms verse by verse, and blessing by blessing, and see if, like the little boy of our story, you are not made to confess that you never knew before "how perfectly splendid God is."

The last verse of the Book of Psalms, taken in connection with the vision of John in the Book of Revelation, is very significant. The psalmist says, "Let everything that hath breath praise the Lord." And in the Book of Revelation, John, who declares himself to be our brother and our companion in tribulation, tells us that he heard this being done. "And every creature which is in heaven, and on the earth, and under the earth, and such as are in the sea, and all that are in them, heard I saying, Blessing, and honor, and glory and power, be unto him that sitteth upon the throne, and unto the Lamb, forever and ever."

The time for universal praise is sure to come some day. Let us begin to do our part now.

I heard once of a discontented, complaining man who, to the great surprise of his friends, became bright, and happy, and full of thanksgiving. After watching him for a little while, and being convinced that the change was permanent, they asked him what had happened. "Oh," he replied, "I have changed my residence. I used to live in Grumbling Lane, but now I have moved into Thanksgiving Square, and I find that I am so rich in blessings that I am always happy."

Shall we each one make this move now?

# Chapter Sixteen - Conformed to the Image of Christ

"For whom he did foreknow, he also did predestinate to be conformed to the image of his Son, that he might be the firstborn among many brethren."

God's ultimate purpose in our creation was that we should finally be "conformed to the image of Christ." Christ was to be the firstborn among many brethren, and His brethren were to be like Him. All the discipline and training of our lives is with this end in view; and God has implanted in every human heart a longing, however unformed and unexpressed, after the best and highest it knows.

Christ is the pattern of what each one of us is to be when finished. We are "predestinated" to be conformed to His image, in order that He might be the firstborn among many brethren. We are to be "partakers of the divine nature" with Christ; we are to be filled with the spirit of Christ; we are to share His resurrection life, and to walk as He walked. We are to be one with Him, as He is one with the Father; and the glory God gave to Him, He is to give to us. And when all this is brought to pass, then, and not until then, will God's purpose in our creation be fully accomplished, and we stand forth "in his image and after his likeness."

Our likeness to His image is an accomplished fact in the mind of God, but we are, so to speak, in the manufactory as yet, and the great master Workman is at work upon us. "It doth not yet appear what we shall be: but we know that, when he shall appear, we shall be like him; for we shall see him as he is."

And so it is written: "The first man Adam was made a living soul; the last Adam was made a quickening spirit. Howbeit that was not first which is spiritual, but that which is natural; and afterward that which is spiritual. The first man is of the earth, earthy; the second man is the Lord from heaven. As is the earthly, such are they also that are earthy; and as is the heavenly, such are they also that are heavenly. And as we have borne the image of the earthly, we shall also bear the image of the heavenly."

It is deeply interesting to see that this process, which was begun in Genesis, is declared to be completed in Revelation, where the "one like unto the Son of man" gave to John this significant message to the overcomers: "Him that overcometh will I make a pillar in the temple of my God; and he shall go no more out: and I will write upon him the name of my God, and the name of the city of my God which is new Jerusalem, which cometh down out of heaven from my God: and I will write upon him my new name." Since name always means character in the Bible, this message can only mean that at last God's purpose is accomplished, and the spiritual evolution of man is completed—he has been made, what God intended from the first, so truly into His likeness and image, as to merit having written upon him the name of God!

Words fail before such a glorious destiny as this! But our Lord foreshadows it in His wonderful prayer when He asks for His brethren that "they all may be one; as thou, Father, art in me, and I in thee, that they also may be one in us: that the world may believe that thou hast sent me. And the glory which thou gavest me I have given them: that they may be one even as we are one. I in them, and thou in me, that they may be made perfect in one." Could oneness be closer or more complete?

Paul also foreshadows this glorious consummation when he declares that if we suffer with Christ we shall also be glorified together with Him, and when he asserts that the "sufferings of this present time are not worthy to be compared with the glory that shall be revealed in us." The whole Creation waits for the revealing of this glory, for Paul goes on to say that the "earnest expectation of the creature waiteth for the manifestation of the sons of God." And he adds finally: "And not only they, but ourselves also, which have the first fruits of the Spirit, even we ourselves groan within ourselves, waiting for the adoption, to wit, the redemption of our body."

In view of such a glorious destiny, at which I dare not do more than hint, shall we not cheerfully welcome the processes, however painful they may be, by which we are to reach it? And shall we not strive eagerly and earnestly to be "laborers together with God" in helping to bring it about? He is the great master Builder, but He wants our co-operation in building up the fabric of our characters, and He exhorts us to take heed how we build. We are all of us at every moment of our lives engaged in this building. Sometimes we build with gold, and silver, and precious stones, and sometimes we build with wood, and hay, and stubble. And we are solemnly warned that every man's work is to be made manifest, "for the day shall declare it, because it shall be revealed by fire." There is no escaping this. We cannot hope, when that day comes, to conceal our wood, and hay, and stubble, however successfully we may have managed to do so beforehand.

To my mind there is no more solemn passage in the whole Bible than the one in Galations which says: "Be not deceived: God is not mocked: for whatsoever a man soweth, that shall he also reap. For he that soweth to the flesh shall of the flesh reap corruption; but he that soweth to the Spirit, shall of the Spirit reap life everlasting." It is the awful inevitableness of this that is so awe-inspiring. It is far worse than any arbitrary punishment; for punishment can sometimes be averted, but there is no possibility of altering the working of a natural law such as this.

In a Catechism I saw were the following questions and answers:

Q. What is the reward for generosity?

A. More generosity.

Q. What is the punishment for meanness?

A. More meanness.

No Catechism ever spoke more truly. We all of us know it for ourselves. In the parable of the talents our Lord illustrates this inevitable law. The condemnation on the unfaithful servant may have sometimes seemed to us unfair, but it was only the reaping of what that servant had sowed. "Take therefore the talent from him and give it unto him which hath ten talents. For unto every one that hath shall be given, and he shall have abundance: but from him that hath not, shall be taken away even that which he hath." This is no arbitrary pronouncement, but is simply a revelation of the inherent nature of things from which none of us can escape.

But in order to be laborers together with God, we must not only build with His materials but also by His processes, and of these we are often very ignorant. Our idea of building is of hard laborious work done in the sweat of our brow; but God's idea is far different. Paul tells us what it is. "We all," he says, "with open face beholding as in a glass the glory of the Lord, are changed into the same image from glory to glory, even as by the Spirit of the Lord." Our work is to "behold," and as we behold the Lord effects the marvelous transformation, and we are "changed into the same image by the Spirit of the Lord." This means, of course, to behold not in our earthly sense of merely looking at a thing, but in the divine sense of really seeing the thing. We are to behold with our spiritual eyes the glory of the Lord, and are to continue beholding it. The glory of the Lord does not mean, however, a great shine or halo. The real glory of the Lord is the glory of what He is and of what He does—the glory of character. And it is this we are to behold.

Let me give an illustration. Someone offends me, and I am tempted to get angry and retaliate. But I look at Christ and think of what He would have done, and dwell upon the thought of His gentleness and meekness and His love for the offending one; and, as I look, I begin to want to be like Him, and I ask in faith that I may be made a "partaker of his nature," and anger and revenge die out of my heart, and I love my enemy and long to serve him.

It is by this sort of beholding Christ that we are to be changed into His image; and the nearer we keep to Him the more rapid the change will be.

I have heard of a wonderful mirror known to science, which is called the parabolic mirror. It is a hollow cone lined with a mirror all over its inside surface. It possesses the power of focusing rays of light in different degrees of intensity in proportion to the increasing nearness to its meeting point at the top end of the cone, the power being more and more intense as the terminal point is approached. It has been discovered by science that at a certain stage in this advance toward the interior point where all the sides of the mirror meet in absolute oneness, the power of the focus concentrates all the light-giving properties of the sun's rays into such an intense brilliancy, as to make visible things never before discerned by the human eye, rendering even flesh transparent, and enabling us to see through the outer covering of our bodies to the inner operations beneath.

Advancing a little farther into the interior of our mirror, the heat properties of the sun's rays are so concentrated as to generate a heat sufficient to melt iron in sixteen seconds, and to dissipate in fourteen seconds the alloy of gold, leaving only the solid globule of the pure metal.

Advancing farther still, the photographing properties of the sunlight are so concentrated as to impress an ineffaceable image of the mirror upon anything that is passed for only one second through the focus.

Advancing still farther, nearly to the point of oneness, the magnetizing powers of light are so concentrated that anything exposed to it for a single instant becomes a powerful magnet, drawing afterward all things to itself.

Whether all this is scientifically correct or not, I am not enough of a scientist to know, but at least it will serve as an allegory to show the progress of the soul as it is changed from glory to glory in its evolution "into his image."

First, as we behold as in a mirror the glory of the Lord, we come to the light focus, which reveals our sinfulness and our need. "Then spake Jesus again unto them, saying, I am the light of the world; he that followeth me shall not walk in darkness, but shall have the light of life."

Second, as we draw closer, we reach the heat focus, where all our dross and reprobate silver is burned up. For He is like a refiner's fire, and like fuller's soap: and "he shall sit as a refiner and purifier of silver; and he shall purify the sons of Levi, and purge them as gold and silver, that they may offer unto the Lord an offering in righteousness."

Third, as we draw closer still, we come to the photographing focus, where the image of Christ is indelibly impressed upon our souls, and we are made like Him because we see Him as He is. "We know that when he shall appear, we shall be like him, for we shall see him as he is."

Fourth and finally, as we come to the point of oneness, we reach the magnetic focus, where our character is so conformed to Christ, that men seeing it will be irresistibly drawn to glorify our Father which is in Heaven.

If we would be conformed to the image of Christ, then we must live closer and ever closer to Him. We must become better and better acquainted with His character and His ways; we must look at things through His eyes, and judge all things by His standards.

It is not by effort or by wrestling that this conformity is to be accomplished; it is by assimilation. According to a natural law, we grow like those with whom we associate, and the stronger character always exercises the controlling influence. And, as divine law is all one with natural law, only working in a higher sphere and with more unhindered power, it need not seem mysterious to us that we should become like Christ by a spiritual union with Him.

But again I must repeat that this union with Christ cannot come by our own efforts, no matter how strenuous they may be. Christ is to "dwell in our hearts by faith," and He can dwell there in no other way. Paul, when he tells us that he was crucified with Christ, says: "Nevertheless I live: yet not I but Christ liveth in me: and the life that I now live, I live by the faith of the Son of God who loved me, and gave himself for me."

"Christ liveth in me," this is the transforming secret. If Christ liveth in me, His life must, in the very nature of things, be manifested in my mortal flesh, and I cannot fail to be changed from glory to glory into His image.

Our Lord's teaching about this is very emphatic. "Abide in me," He says, "and I in you. As the branch cannot bear fruit of itself except it abide in the vine; no more can ye, except ye abide in me. I am the vine, ye are the branches. He that abideth in me, and I in him, the same bringeth forth much fruit; for without me ye can do nothing."

This is literally true. If we abide in Him, and He in us, we can no more help bring forth fruit than can the branches of a flourishing vine. In the very nature of things the fruit must come.

But we cannot take the "old man" into Christ. We must put off the old man with his deeds before we can "put on the Lord Jesus Christ." And the apostle, in writing to the Colossians, bases his exhortations to holiness of life on the fact that they had done this. "Lie not one to another," he says, "seeing that ye have put off the old man with his deeds, and have put on the new man, which is renewed in knowledge after the image of him that created him."

Sin must disappear at the incoming of Christ; and no soul that is not prepared to surrender all that is contrary to His will can hope to welcome Him. The "old man" must be put off if the new man is to reign. But both the putting off and the putting on must be done by faith. There is no other way. As I have tried to explain elsewhere, we must move our personality, our ego, our will out of self and into Christ. We must reckon ourselves to be dead to self, and alive only to God. "Reckon ye also yourselves to be dead indeed unto sin, but alive unto God through Jesus Christ our Lord." "Neither yield ye your members as instruments of unrighteousness unto sin; but yield yourselves unto God as those that are alive from the dead, and your members as instruments of righteousness unto God."

The same kind of reckoning of faith, which brings the forgiveness of sins within our grasp, brings also this union with Christ. To those who do not understand the law of faith, this will no doubt be as great a mystery as the secrets of gravitation were before the law of gravitation was discovered; but, to those who understand it, the law of faith works as unerringly and as definitely as the law of gravitation, and produces its results as certainly. No one can read the seventh chapter of Hebrews and fail to see that faith is an all-conquering force. I believe myself it is the creative force of the universe. It is the higher law that controls all the lower laws beneath it; and what looks like a miracle is simply the working of this higher controlling law.

Faith is, as I say, the law of Creation. "Through faith we understand that the worlds were framed by the word of God, so that things which are seen were not made of things which are seen were not made of things which do appear." We are told that "God spake and it was done, he commanded and it stood fast." And our Lord tells us that if we have faith we can do the same. "And Jesus answering saith unto them, Have faith in God. For verily I say unto you, That whosoever shall say unto this mountain, Be thou removed, and be thou cast into the sea, and shall not doubt in his heart, but shall believe that those things which he saith shall come to pass, he shall have whatsoever he saith. Therefore I say unto you, What things soever ye desire when ye pray, believe that ye receive them, and ye shall have them."

Faith, we are told, calls those things which be not as though they were; and, in so calling them, brings them into being. Therefore, although we cannot see any tangible sign of change when by faith we put off the old man, which is corrupt according to the deceitful lusts, and by faith put on the new man which after God is created in righteousness and true holiness, yet nevertheless, it has really been done, and faith has accomplished it. I cannot explain this theologically, but I can fearlessly assert that it is a tremendous practical reality; and that those souls who abandon the self-life, and give themselves up the Lord to be fully possessed by Him, do find that He takes possession of the inner springs of their being, and works there to will and to do of His good pleasure.

Paul prayed for the Ephesians that "Christ might dwell in their hearts by faith," and this is the whole secret of being conformed to His image. If Christ is dwelling in my heart I must necessarily be Christlike. I cannot be unkind, or irritable, or self-seeking, or dishonest; but His gentleness, and sweetness, and tender compassion, and loving submission to the will of His Father must be manifested in my daily walk and conversation.

We shall not be fully changed into the image of Christ until He shall appear, and we shall "see him as he is." But meanwhile, according to our measure, the life of Jesus is to be made "manifest in our mortal flesh." Is it made manifest in ours? Are we so "conformed to the image" of Christ that men in seeing us see a glimpse of Him also?

A Methodist minister's wife told me that at one time, when they had moved to a new place, her little boy came in after the first afternoon of play, and exclaimed joyfully, "Oh, Mother, I have found such a lovely, good little girl to play with, that I never want to go away again."

"I am very glad, darling," said the loving mother, happy over her child's happiness. "What is the little girl's name?"

"Oh," replied the child, with a sudden solemnity, "I think her name is Jesus."

"Why, Frank!" exclaimed the horrified mother, "what do you mean?"

"Well, Mother," he said deprecatingly, "she was so lovely that I did not know what she could be called but Jesus."

Are our lives so Christlike that anyone could have such a thought of us? Is it patent to all around us that we have been with Jesus? Is it not, alas, often just the contrary? Are not some of us so cross and uncomfortable in our living that exactly the opposite thing would have to be said about us?

Paul says we are to be "epistles of Christ," known and read of all men, "written, not with ink, but with the Spirit of the living God, not in tables of stone, but in fleshy tables of the heart." I firmly believe that if every child of God, all the world over, would begin from this day onward to be an "epistle of Christ," living a truly Christlike life at home and abroad, it would not be a month before the churches would all be crowded with inquirers, coming in to see what was the religion that could so transform human nature into something divine.

The world is full of unbelievers in the reality of the Christian religion, and nothing will convince them but facts which they cannot disprove. We must meet them with transformed lives. If they see that whereas once we were cross, now we are sweet; once we were proud, now we are humble; once we were fretful, now we are patient and calm; and if we are able to testify that it is the religion of Christ that has wrought this change, they cannot help but be impressed.

A Christian man who, on account of his earnest work, had gained a great reputation for piety, had unfortunately gained an equally great reputation for a bad temper and a sharp tongue. But at last, for some reason which no one could understand, a change seemed to come over him, and his temper and his tongue became as sweet and as gentle as they had before been violent and sharp. His friends watched and wondered, and at last one of them approached him on the subject, and asked him if he had changed his religion. "No," replied the man, "I have not changed my religion, but I have at last let my religion change me."

How much has our religion changed us?

It is very easy to have a church religion, or a prayer meeting religion, or a Christian-work religion; but it is altogether a different thing to have an everyday religion. To "show piety at home" is one of the most vital parts of Christianity, but it is also one far too rare; and it is not at all an uncommon thing to find Christians who "do their righteousness" before outsiders "to be seen of men," but who fail lamentably in showing their piety at home. I knew a father of a family who was so powerful in prayer at the weekly prayer meeting, and so impressive in exhortation that the whole church was much edified by his piety; but who, when he went home after the meetings, was so cross and ugly that his wife and family were afraid to say a word in his presence.

"And when thou prayest, thou shalt not be as the hypocrites are; for they love to pray standing in the synagogues and in the corners of the streets, that they may be seen of men. Verily I say unto you, They have their reward." These words, "They have their reward," seem to me among the most solemn in the Bible. What we do to be seen of men is seen of men, and that is all there is to it. There is no conformity to the image of Christ in this sort of righteousness that bears everyday trials cheerfully, and is patient under home provacations; that returns good for evil, and meets all the homely friction of daily life with sweetness and gentleness; that suffereth long and is kind; that envieth not; that flaunteth not itself; that is not puffed up; that seeketh not its own; is not easily provoked; and thinketh no evil; that beareth all things, believeth all things, hopeth all things, endureth all things. This is what it means to be conformed to the image of Christ! Do we know anything of such righteousness as this?

We sometimes talk about performing what we call our "religious duties," meaning by this expression our church services, or our stated seasons of devotion, or our Christian work of one sort or another; and we never dream that it is far more our "religious duty" to be Christlike in our daily walk and conversation than to be faithful even in these other things, desirable as they may be in themselves.

The righteousness of the scribes and Pharisees was a righteousness of words and phrases and of ceremonial observances, and this is often very impressive to outsiders. But, because it was nothing more, our Lord condemns it in unmeasured terms: "Woe unto you, scribes and Pharisees, hypocrites! For ye pay tithe of mint and anise, and cummin, and have omitted the weightier matters of the law, judgment, mercy, and faith: these ought ye to have done, and not to leave the other undone. Woe unto you, scribes and Pharisees, hypocrites! For ye are like unto whited sepulchers, which indeed appear beautiful outward, but are within full of dead men's bones, and of all uncleanness." And He adds: "Even so ye also outwardly appear righteous unto men, but within ye are full of hypocrisy and iniquity."

It is very easy to say beautiful things about the religious life, but to be what we say is an altogether different matter. I know a Sunday school teacher who had been teaching her scholars a great deal about casting all your cares on the Lord, and trusting Him in times of trial; and they had been very much impressed. But at last a trouble came into the life of this teacher, and some of her scholars saw her in her own home while it lasted. To their amazement and distress they saw her fretting, and chafing, and worrying, and complaining, acting, in short, just as if there was no God to trust, or as if His ways were not ways of love and goodness. It was all "object lesson" to those children that undid all the good which that teacher's previous teaching had seemed likely to accomplish; and one of them, who was very observant, said to me triumphantly, "I thought it could not be true while Miss ____ was telling us about how we might trust the Lord for everything; and now I see it was only goody talk, for she doesn't do it herself."

A cross Christian, or an anxious one, a discouraged gloomy Christian, a doubting Christian, a complaining Christian, an exacting Christian, a selfish, cruel, hardhearted Christian, a self-indulgent Christian, a Christian with a sharp tongue or a bitter spirit; a Christian, in short, who is not Christlike may preach to the winds with as much hope of success, as to preach to his own family or friends, who see him as he is. There is no escape from this inevitable law of things, and we may as well recognize it at once. If we want our loved ones to trust the Lord, volumes of talk about it will not be one-thousandth part as convincing to them as the sight of a little real trust on our own part in the time of need. The longest prayer and the loudest preaching are of no avail in any family circle, however they may do in the pulpit, unless there is on the part of the preacher a living out of the things preached.

Some Christians seem to think that the fruits which the Bible calls for are some form of outward religious work, such as holding meetings, visiting the poor, conduction charitable institutions, and so forth. Whereas the fact is that the Bible scarcely mentions these at all as fruits of the Spirit, but declares that the fruit of the Spirit is love, joy, peace, long-suffering, gentleness, goodness, faith, meekness, temperance. A Christlike character must necessarily be the fruit of Christ's indwelling. Other things will no doubt be the outcome of this character; but first and foremost comes the character, or all the rest is but a hollow sham. A late writer has said: "A man can never be more than his character makes him. A man can never do more nor better than deliver or embody that which his character. Nothing valuable can come out of a man that is not first in the man. Character must stand behind and back up everything—the sermon, the poem, the picture, the book. None of them is worth a straw without it."

In order to become conformed to the image of Christ, we must of necessity be made "partakers of the divine nature." And, where this is the case, that divine nature must necessarily manifest itself. Our tastes, our wishes, our purposes will become like Christ's tastes, and wishes, and purposes; we shall change eyes with Him, and see things as He sees them. This is inevitable; for where the divine nature is, its fruits cannot fail to be manifest; and, where they are not manifest, we are forced to conclude that that individual, no matter how loud his professions, has not yet been made a partaker of the divine nature.

I can hear someone asking, But do you really mean to say that, in order to be made partakers of the divine nature, we must cease from our own efforts entirely, and must simply by faith put on Christ, and must let Him live in us and work in us to will and to do of His good pleasure? And do you believe He will then actually do it?

To this I answer most emphatically, Yes, I mean just that. I mean that if we abandon ourselves entirely to Him, He comes to abide in us, and is Himself our life. We must commit our whole lives to Him, our thoughts, our words, our daily walk, our downsittings, our uprisings. By faith we must abandon ourselves, and, as it were, move over into Christ, and abide in Him. By faith we must put off the old man, and by faith we must put on the new man. By faith we must reckon ourselves dead unto sin, and alive unto God; as truly dead as alive. By faith we must realize that our daily life is Christ living in us; and, ceasing from our own works, we must suffer Him to work in us to will and to do of His good pleasure. It is no longer truth about Him that must fill our hearts, but it is Himself—the living, loving, glorious Christ—who will, if we let Him, in very deed make us His dwelling place, and who will reign and rule within us, and "subdue all things unto himself." "Therefore if any man be in Christ, he is a new creature; old things are passed away; behold, all things are become new."

It was no mere figure of speech when our Lord in that wonderful Sermon on the Mount said to His disciples: "Be ye therefore perfect even as your Father in heaven is perfect." He meant, of course, according to our measure, but He meant that reality of being conformed to His image to which we have been predestined. And in the Epistle to the Hebrews we are shown how it is to be brought about. "Now the God of peace, that brought again from the dead our Lord Jesus, that great Shepherd of the sheep, through the blood of the everlasting covenant, make you perfect in every good work to do his will; working in you that which is well pleasing in His sight, through Jesus Christ: to whom be glory forever and ever. Amen."

It is to be by His working in us, and not by our working in ourselves, that this purpose of God in our creation is to be accomplished; and if it should look as regards some of us that we are too far removed from any conformity to the image of Christ for such a transformation ever to be wrought, we must remember that our Maker is not finished making us yet. The day will come, if we do not hinder, when the work begun in Genesis shall be finished in Revelation, and the whole Creation, as well as ourselves, shall be delivered from the bondage of corruption into the glorious liberty of the children of God.

"For we know that the whole creation groaneth and travaileth in pain together until now. And not only they, but ourselves also, which have the first fruits of the Spirit, even we ourselves groan within ourselves, waiting for the adoption, to wit the redemption of our body."

*'Tis, shall Thy will be done for me? or mine,*
*And I be made a thing, not after Thine;*
*My own, and full of paltriest pretense?*
*Shall I be born of God, or of mere man?*
*Be made like Christ, or on some other plan?*
*What though Thy work in me transcends my sense,*
*Too fine, too high for me to understand.*
*I trust entirely. Oh, Lord, with Thy labor grand!*
*I have not knowledge, wisdom, insight, thought,*
*Nor understanding fit to justify*
*Thee in Thy work, O Perfect. Thou hast brought*
*Me up to this, and lo! what thou hast wrought*
*I cannot call it good. But I can cry*
*"O enemy, the Maker hath not done;*
*One day thou shalt behold, and from the sight wilt run."*

# Chapter Seventeen - God Is Enough

"My soul wait thou only upon God, for my expectation is from him. He only is my rock and my salvation; he is my defense; I shall not be moved. In God is my salvation, and my glory: the rock of my strength and my refuge is in God."

The last and greatest lesson that the soul has to learn is the fact that God, and God alone, is enough for all its needs. This is the lesson that all His dealings with us are meant to teach; and this is the crowning discovery of our whole Christian life. God is enough!

We have been considering in this book some aspects of the character and the ways of God as revealed to us in the Lord Jesus Christ; and also some of the mistakes which prevent us from appropriating the fullness that is ours in Him. And now in conclusion I want to tell, as best I can, what seems to me the outcome of the whole matter.

If God is what He would seem to be from the revealings we have been considering; if He is indeed the "God of all comfort," as we have seen; if He is our Shepherd; if He is really and truly our Father; if, in short, all the many aspects we have been studying of His character and His ways are actually true, then we must, it seems to me, come to the positive conviction that He is, in Himself alone, enough for all our possible needs, and that we may safely rest in Him absolutely and forever.

Most Christians have, I suppose, sung more often than they could count, these words in one of our most familiar hymns:

*Thou, O Christ, art all I want,*
*More than all in Thee I find.*

But I doubt whether all of us could honestly say that the words have expressed any reality in our own experience. Christ has not been all we want. We have wanted a great many things besides Him. We have wanted fervent feelings about Him, or realizations of His presence with us, or an interior revelation of His love; or else we have demanded satisfactory schemes of doctrine, or successful Christian work, or something of one sort or another, besides Himself, that will constitute a personal claim upon Him. Just Christ Himself, Christ alone, without the addition of any of our experiences concerning Him, has not been enough for us in spite of all our singing; and we do not even see how it is possible that He could be enough.

The psalmist said in those old days: "My soul, wait thou only upon God: for my expectation is from him." But now the Christian says, "My soul, wait thou upon my sound doctrines, for my expectation is from them"; or, "My soul, wait thou on my good disposition and feelings, or upon my righteous works, or upon my fervent prayers, or upon my earnest striving, for my expectation is from these." To wait upon God only seems one of the unsafest things they can do, and to have their expectation from Him alone is like building on the sand. They reach out on every side for something to depend on, and, not until everything else fails, will they put their trust in God alone. George Macdonald says: "We look upon God as our last and feeblest resource. We only go to Him when we have nowhere else to go. And then we learn that the storms of life have driven us, not upon the rocks, but into the desired haven."

No soul can be really at rest until it has given up all dependence on everything else and has been forced to depend on the Lord alone. As long as our expectation is from other things, nothing but disappointment awaits us. Feelings may change, and will change with our changing circumstances; doctrines and dogmas may be upset; Christian work may come to naught; prayers may seem to lose their fervency; promises may seem to fail; everything that we have believed in or depended upon may seem to be swept away, and only God is left, just God, the bare God, if I may be allowed the expression; simply and only God.

We say sometimes, "If I could only find a promise to fit my case, I could then be at rest." But promises may be misunderstood or misapplied, and, at the moment when we are leaning all our weight upon them, they may seem utterly to fail us. But the Promiser, who is behind His promises, and is infinitely more than His promises, can never fail nor change. The little child does not need to have any promises from its mother to make it content; it has its mother herself, and she is enough. Its mother is better than a thousand promises. In our highest ideal of love or friendship, promises do not enter. One party may love to make promises, just as our Lord does, but the other party does not need them; the personality of lover or friend is better than all their promises. And should every promise be wiped out of the Bible, we would still have God left, and God would be enough. Again I repeat it, only God, He Himself, just as He is, without the addition of anything on our part, whether it be disposition or feelings, or experiences, or good works, or sound doctrines, or any other thing either outward or inward. "God only is my rock and my salvation; he is my defense: I shall not be moved."

I do not mean by this that we are not to have feelings, or experiences, or revelations, or good works, or sound doctrines. We may have all of these, but they must be the result of salvation, and never the procuring cause; and they can never be depended upon as being any indication of our spiritual condition. They are all things that come and go, and are dependent often upon the state of our health, or the condition of our surroundings, or even sometimes upon the quarter of the wind. Some people, for instance, can never believe that God loves them when the wind is in slightest degree as the groundwork for our confidence or our joy, we are sure to come to grief. What I do mean is that we are to hold ourselves absolutely independent of them all, resting in only the grand, magnificent fact that God is, and that He is our Saviour; our inner life prospers just as well and is just as triumphant without these personal experiences or personal doings as it is with them. We are to find God, the fact of God, sufficient for all our spiritual needs, whether we feel ourselves to be in a desert or in a fertile valley. We are to say with the prophet: "Although the fig-tree shall not blossom, neither shall fruit be in the vines; the labor of the olive shall fail, and the field shall yield no meat, the flock shall be cut off from the fold, and there shall be no herd in the stall; yet I will rejoice in the Lord, I will joy in the God of my salvation."

The soul is made for this, and can never find rest short of it. All God's dealings with us, therefore, are shaped to this end; and He is often obliged to deprive us of all joy in everything else in order that He may force us to find our joy only and altogether in Himself. It is all very well, perhaps, to rejoice in His promises, or to rejoice in the revelations He may have granted us, or in the experiences we may have realized; but to rejoice in the Promiser Himself—Himself alone—without promises, or experiences, or revelations, this is crowning point of Christian life; and this is the only place where we can know the peace which passes all understanding, and which nothing can disturb.

It is difficult to explain just what I mean. We have so accustomed ourselves to consider all these accompaniments of the spiritual life as being the spiritual life itself that it is hard to detach ourselves from them. We cannot think that the Lord can be anything to us unless we find in ourselves something to assure us of His love and His care. And when we talk about finding our all in Him, we generally mean that we find it in our feelings or our views about Him. If, for instance, we feel a glow of love toward Him, then we can say heartily that He is enough; but when this glow fails, as sooner or later it is almost sure to do, then we no longer feel that we have found our all in Him. The truth is that what satisfies us is not the Lord, but our own feelings about the Lord. But we are not conscious of this; and consequently when our feelings fail we think it is the Lord who has failed, and we are plunged into darkness.

Of course, all this is very foolish, but it is such a common experience that very few can see how foolish it is. Perhaps an illustration may help us to clearer vision. Let us think of a man accused of a crime, standing before a judge. Which would be the thing of moment for that man: his own feelings toward the judge, or the judge's feelings toward him? Would he spend his time watching his own emotions, and trying to see whether he felt that the judge was favorable to him or would he watch the judge and try to discover from his looks or his words whether or not to expect a favorable judgment? Of course we will say at once that the man's own feelings are not of the slightest account in the matter, and that only the opinions and feelings of the judge are worth a moment's thought. The man might have all the "glows" and all the "experiences" conceivable, but these would avail absolutely nothing. Upon the judge only would everything depend.

This is what we would call a self-evident fact.

In the same way, if we will only bring our common sense to bear upon the subject, we cannot help seeing that the only really vital thing in our relations with the Lord is, not what are our feelings toward Him, but what are His feelings toward us. The man who is being tried must find in the judge all he needs, if he is to find it at all. His sufficiency cannot possibly be of himself, but it must be of the one upon whom his fate depends. And our sufficiency, the apostle says, is not of ourselves but of God.

This, then, is what I mean by God being enough. It is that we find in Him, in the fact of His existence, and of His character, all that we can possibly want for everything. God is, must be our answer to every question and every cry of need. If there is any lack in the One who has undertaken to save us, nothing supplementary we can do will avail to make it up; and if there is no lack in Him, then He, of Himself and in Himself, is enough.

I wish it were possible to make my meaning plain, for I believe it is the secret of permanent deliverance from all the discomfort and unrest of every Christian life. Your discomfort and unrest arise from your strenuous but useless efforts to get up some satisfactory basis of confidence within yourselves; such, for instance, as what you consider to be the proper feelings, or the right amount of fervor or earnestness, or at least, if nothing else, a sufficient degree of interest in spiritual matters. And because none of these things are ever satisfactory (and, I may tell you, never will be), it is impossible for your religious life to be anything but uncomfortable.

But if we see that all our salvation from beginning to end depends on the Lord alone; and if we have learned that He is able and willing to do for us "exceeding abundantly above all we can ask or think," then peace and comfort cannot fail to reign supreme. Everything depends upon whether the Lord, in and of Himself, is enough for our salvation, or whether other things must be added on our part to make Him sufficient.

The thing that helped me personally more than anything else to come to a conviction that God was really enough for me was an experience I had some years ago. It was at a time in my religious life when I was passing through a great deal of questioning and perplexity, and I felt that no Christian had ever had such peculiar difficulties as mine before. There happened to be staying near me just then for a few weeks a lady who was considered to be a deeply spiritual Christian, and to whom I had been advised to apply for spiritual help. I summoned up my courage, therefore, one afternoon and went to see her, pouring out my troubles; I expected of course that she would take a deep interest in me, and would be at great pains to do all she could to help me.

She listened patiently enough, and did not interrupt me; but when I had finished my story, and had paused, expecting sympathy and consideration, she simply said, "Yes, all you say may be very true, but then, in spite of it all, there is God." I waited a few minutes for something more, but nothing came, and my friend and teacher had the air of having said all that was necessary.

"But," I continued, "surely you did not understand how very serious and perplexing my difficulties are."

"Oh, yes, I did," replied my friend, "but then, as I tell you, there is God." And I could not induce her to make any other answer. It seemed to me most disappointing and unsatisfactory. I felt that my peculiar and really harrowing experiences could not be met by anything so simple as merely the statement, "Yes, but there is God." I knew God was there, of course, but I felt I needed something more than just God; and I came to the conclusion that my friend, for all her great reputation as a spiritual teacher, was at any rate not able to grapple with a peculiar case such as mine.

However, my need was so great that I did not give up with my first trial, but went to her again and again, always with the hope that she would sometime begin to understand the importance of my difficulties and would give me adequate help. It was of no avail. I was never able to draw forth any other answer. Always to everything would come the simple reply, with an air of entirely dismissing the subject, "Yes, I know; but there is God." And at last by dint of her continual repetition I became convinced that my friend really and truly believed that the mere fact of the existence of God, as the Creator and Redeemer of mankind, and of me as a member of the race, was an all-sufficient answer to every possible need of His creatures. And at last, because she said it so often and seemed so sure, I began dimly to wonder whether after all God might not be enough, even for my need, overwhelming and secular as I felt it to be. From wondering I came gradually to believing, that, being my Creator and Redeemer, He must be enough; and at last a conviction burst upon me that He really was enough, and my eyes were opened to the fact of the absolute and utter all-sufficiency of God.

My troubles disappeared like magic, and I did nothing but wonder how I could ever have been such an idiot as to be troubled by them, when all the while there was God, the Almighty and all-seeing God, the God who had created me, and was therefore on my side, and eager to care for me and help me. I had found out that God was enough and my soul was at rest.

The all-sufficiency of God ought to be as complete to the child of God as the all-sufficiency of a good mother is to the child of that mother. We all know the utter rest of the little child in the mother's presence and the mother's love. That its mother is there is enough to make all fears and all troubles disappear. It does not need the mother to make any promises; she herself, just as she is, without promises and without explanations, is all that the child needs.

My own experience as a child taught me this, beyond any possibility of question. My mother was the remedy for all my own ills, and, I fully believed, for the ills of the whole world, if only they could be brought to her. And when anyone expressed doubts as to her capacity to remedy everything, I remembered with what fine scorn I used to annihilate them, by saying, "Ah! but you don't know my mother."

And now, when any tempest-tossed soul fails to see that God is enough, I feel like saying, not with scorn, but with infinite pity, "Ah, dear friend, you do not know God! Did you know Him, you could not help seeing that He is the remedy for every need of your soul, and that He is an all-sufficient remedy. God is enough, even though no promise may seem to fit your case, nor any inward assurance give you confidence. The Promiser is more than His promises; and His existence is a surer ground of confidence than the most fervent inward feelings."

*Oh, utter but the name of God*
*Down in the heart of hearts,*
*And see how from the soul at once*
*All anxious fear departs.*

But someone may say, "All this is no doubt true, and I could easily believe it, if I could only be sure it applied to me. But I am so good-for-nothing and so full of sin, that I do not feel as if I had any claim to such riches of grace."

All the more, if you are good-for-nothing and full of sin, have you a claim on the all-sufficiency of God. Your very good-for-nothingness and sinfulness are your loudest claims. As someone has said, it is only the sinner that wants salvation who stands in the Saviour's path. And the Bible declares that Christ Jesus came into the world to save sinners; not to save the righteous, not to save the fervent, not to save the earnest workers, but simply and only to save sinners. Why then should we spend our time and energies in trying to create a claim, which after all is no claim, but only a hindrance.

As long as our attention is turned upon ourselves and our own experiences, just so long is it turned away from the Lord. This is plain common sense. As I have said elsewhere, we can only see the thing we look at, and while we are looking at ourselves, we simply cannot "behold God." It is not that He hides Himself; He is always there in full view of all who look unto Him; but if we are looking in another direction, we cannot expect to see Him.

Heretofore, it may be, our eyes have been so fixed upon ourselves that all our interior questioning has been simply and only as regarded our own condition. Is my love for God warm enough? Am I enough in earnest? Are my feeling toward Him what they ought to be? Have I enough zeal? Do I feel my need as I ought? And we have been miserable because we have never been able to answer these questions satisfactorily. Although we do not know it, it has been a mercy we never could answer them satisfactorily, for, if we had, the self in us would have been exalted, and we should have been filled with self-congratulation and pride.

If we want to see God, our interior questioning must be, not about ourselves, but about Him. How does God feel toward me? Is His love for me warm enough? Has He enough zeal? Does He feel my need deeply enough? Is He sufficiently in earnest? Although these questions may seem irreverent to some, they simply embody the doubts and fears of a great many doubting hearts, and they only need to be asked in order to prove the fact that these doubts and fears are in themselves the real irreverence. We all know what would be the triumphant answers to such questions. No doubts could withstand their testimony; and the soul that asks and answers them honestly will be shut up to a profound and absolute conviction that God is and must be enough.

"All things are yours," declares the apostle, "whether Paul, or Apollos, or Cephas, or the world, or life, or death, or things present, or things to come; all are yours; and ye are Christ's; and Christ is God's." It would be impossible for any statement to be more all-embracing. And all things are yours because you belong to Christ, not because you are so good and so worthy, but simply and only because you belong to Christ. All things we need are part of our inheritance in Him, and they only await our claiming. Let our needs and difficulties be as great as they may, there is in these "all things" a supply exceeding abundantly above all we can ask or think.

Because He is, all must go right for us. Because the mother is, all must go right, up to the measure of her ability, for her children; and infinitely more must this be true of the Lord. To the child there is, behind all that changes and can change, the one unchangeable fact of the mother's existence. While the mother lives, the child must be cared for; and, while God lives, His children must be cared for as well. What else could He do, being what He is? Neglect, indifference, forgetfulness, ignorance are all impossible to Him. He knows everything, He cares about everything, He can manage everything, and He loves us. What more could we ask?

God's saints in all ages have known this, and have realized that God was enough for them. Job said out of the depths of sorrows and trials, which few can equal,

"Though he slay me, yet will I trust in him." David could say in the moment of his keenest anguish, "yea, though I walk through the valley of the shadow of death," yet "I will fear no evil, for thou art with me." And again he could say: "God is our refuge and strength, a very present help in trouble. Therefore will not we fear though the earth be removed, and though the mountains be carried into the midst of the sea; though the waters thereof roar and be troubled; though the mountains shake with the swelling thereof ... God is in the midst of her; she shall not be moved; God shall help her, and that right early."

Paul could say triumphantly in the midst of many and grievous trials: "For I am persuaded that neither death, nor life, nor angels, nor principalities, nor powers, nor things present, nor things to come, nor height, nor depth, nor any other creature, shall be able to separate us from the love of God, which is in Christ Jesus our Lord."

Therefore, O doubting and sorrowful Christian hearts, in the face of all we have learned concerning the God of all comfort, cannot your realize with Job, and David, and Paul, and the saints of all ages that nothing else is needed to quiet all your fears, but just this, that God is. His simple existence is all the warrant your need requires for its certain relieving. Nothing can separate you from His love, absolutely nothing, neither death nor life, nor angels, nor principalities, nor powers, nor things present, nor things to come, nor height, nor depth, nor any other creature. Every possible contingency is provided for here; and not one of them can separate you from the love of God which is in Christ Jesus our Lord.

After such a declaration as this, how can any of us dare to question or doubt God's love? And, since He loves us, He cannot exist and fail to help us. Do we not know by our own experience what an imperative necessity it is for love to pour itself out in blessing on the ones it loves; and can we not understand that God, who is love, who is, if I may say so, made out of love, simply cannot help blessing us. We do not need to beg Him to bless us, He simply cannot help it.

Therefore God is enough! God is enough for time, God is enough for eternity. God is enough!

*Only to sit and think of God,*
*Oh, what a joy it is!*
*To think the thought, to breathe the name*
*Earth has no higher bliss.*

Made in the USA
Monee, IL
07 June 2020

32764619R10085